businessbuddies

successful
conflict
resolution

For further success in all aspects of
business, be sure to read these other
businessbuddies books:

businessbuddies

successful
conflict
resolution

Ken Lawson, M.A., Ed.M.

First edition for the United States, its territories and dependencies, and Canada
published 2007 by Barron's Educational Series, Inc.

Conceived and created by
Axis Publishing Limited
8c Accommodation Road
London NW11 8ED
www.axispublishing.co.uk

Creative Director: Siân Keogh
Editorial Director: Anne Yelland
Design: Sean Keogh, Simon de Lotz
Consulting Editor: Ken Lawson
Production: Jo Ryan

All inquiries should be addressed to:
Barron's Educational Series, Inc.
250 Wireless Boulevard
Hauppauge, New York 11788
www.barronseduc.com

Library of Congress Control No: 2006932207

ISBN-13: 978-0-7641-3705-1
ISBN-10: 0-7641-3705-0

Printed and bound in China
9 8 7 6 5 4 3 2 1

contents

6

Introduction

If you think you can live and work in a world without conflict, think again. No matter how respectful, caring, and disciplined you are, no matter how much you care about the concerns of people around you, conflict is unavoidable. Is that a bad thing? Not necessarily.

Conflict is always a distraction. At its worst, workplace conflict can be disruptive, demoralizing, and counterproductive. But it can also be a healthy by-product of talent and creativity. In fact, it can shape positive change. Whatever its face, origin, or character, conflict is inevitable. What matters to you is not so much the existence of conflict as how you respond to it. In this book, you'll find a wealth of strategies and guidelines for managing and resolving workplace conflict effectively.

Successful Conflict Resolution shows you the many sides of disagreement and opposition in the workplace—and what to do about them. The opening chapter provides an overview of conflict and its sources, and insights on the interpersonal dynamics of distinctly different personality types. You'll read about common situational sources of conflict, and how they exert influence in the workplace. And, you'll learn what behaviors and activities can result in team conflict.

Chapter 2 looks at how conflict impacts the workplace. Although its overt consequences can be obvious, hidden consequences can be even more damaging. You'll gain perspectives on the costs of conflict—and why many managers ignore them. And you'll learn about the potential benefits of conflict to an organization and its culture.

In Chapter 3, *Successful Conflict Resolution* outlines typical scenarios for conflict in the workplace, and shows how to anticipate them. You'll encounter the different behaviors of conflict and learn how to handle them. You'll also learn how to train staff to manage conflict, how to build team spirit, and how to motivate staff during times of change.

Introduction continued

The principal barriers to conflict resolution are addressed in Chapter 4. You'll gain an understanding of the symptoms of and reasons for such conflict-related behaviors as denial and avoidance, aggression, accommodation, and compromise. You'll also learn about the impact of poor communication, emotionality, undefined job expectations, and misinterpreted motivations.

Chapter 5 provides actionable strategies for resolving conflict and promotes collaboration as the most powerful response to workplace differences. You'll find useful guidelines for sharpening your collaborative skills and helping others do the same. You'll also find many tips for developing listening skills and speaking skills—tools that will enable you to address and manage conflict effectively, and without fear. And, you'll benefit from a step-by-step blueprint that shows collaboration in action, as well as perspectives on how you can model it.

The final chapter covers mediation and how to make it work. You'll contrast mediation with arbitration and learn where and why each is appropriate as an intervention. The chapter explains the benefits of mediation, and the many considerations managers need to keep in mind when choosing to pursue it as a conflict-resolution strategy.

Workplace conflict is unavoidable. But armed with the strategies outlined in this book, there's no longer any need to avoid confronting it. In reader-friendly language and with clear, understandable guidelines, *Successful Conflict Resolution* provides you with the arsenal of tools you'll need to respond to, manage, and conquer workplace conflict.

Ken Lawson, M.A., Ed.M.
Career Management Consultant
New York

1

defining conflict

defining conflict

What is conflict?

Conflicts in the workplace typically occur between two people, but there is no actual limit to the number of people who can be involved (see below). As a manager, it will be up to you to maintain a harmonious workplace among your staff.

How you address issues important to the people who work for you, will have significant impact on your team's productivity and performance. Some of the varying types of conflicts that you need to understand include:

1 OPPOSING FORCES
Conflicts most commonly occur between two people but there is no actual limit to the number of people involved. Three or more people can easily be fighting for the same goal. Various members of a team can also be involved.

2 STRUGGLE
The nature of the struggle (also described as a "dispute" or "disagreement") can arise from a set of different beliefs, desires, actions, or objectives. They can also be the result of a personality clash.

3 WISH FOR SUPREMACY
Often, the two parties may have the same objective, for instance, to become the leader of the group. Even when one of the candidates is named the official leader, the conflict doesn't necessarily stop as the losing aspirant may refuse emotionally to accept the result. Essentially, people who perceive scenarios as necessarily having a winner and a loser (as opposed to two winners) are far more likely to be involved in conflict because the pressure to achieve the status of "winner" is so great.

What is conflict? continued

4

LACK OF COMPROMISE
Most conflicts arise because both parties are trying to force the other to accept their conditions without showing any willingness to compromise or to negotiate.

5

STRONG NEEDS, CONCERNS
When people have powerful needs to accomplish something but face major obstacles, then they face a potential conflict.

6

THREAT OF LOSING
A person facing the possibility of not achieving their objectives because of another person's actions or beliefs is in a state of conflict.

7 LIMITED OPTIONS, RESOURCES
Conflict is also fed by a limited number of resources and options available in a workplace, forcing people (often wrongly) to feel they have to fight against each other to make the most of these resources.

8 FREQUENT INTERACTION
Whether threats are real or not, the more often people interact with each other, the greater the chances are for people to rub each other the wrong way. Frequent interaction is necessary in most workplaces, which is why an office is potentially a breeding ground for conflict.

9 INTERDEPENDENCY
In the workplace, people need to work together. They have no other option. This interdependency heightens the individual pressures both parties may already be feeling.

Myths about conflict

There are several widespread misconceptions about conflict that are important to outline.

1 CONFLICT IS AVOIDABLE

It would be a disservice to state that this book or any other guide will help you avoid conflict. Disagreements are inevitable in the workplace. They are the natural outcome of human interaction. People have different attitudes, beliefs, and expectations, even when they have been educated and brought up in the same place and in the same way. It is natural and healthy for people to have varying opinions and approaches to business.

2

CONFLICT IS NEGATIVE

Many people are brought up to think that conflict is a bad thing. But this is not necessarily true. For instance, the absence of conflict in an office could indicate three things:

■ AUTHORITARIAN REGIME
A top-down management that insists on imposing one way of working and a subdued workforce that doesn't dare to question working practices.

■ LACK OF COMMITMENT
A workforce that never questions assumptions made by managers and never volunteers ideas or alternative thoughts could indicate a lack of engagement and commitment with the company.

■ LACK OF IMAGINATION
Workers who make no input to the company also suggest a dearth of imagination and initiative. This in itself is harmful to a business.

Myths about conflict continued

In fact, conflict is in many ways desirable for the following reasons:

1 HELP TO SOLVE PROBLEMS

Conflict can improve problem solving because it forces people to tackle an issue that has been neglected for a long time, causing potential harm to the company. For example, a bully at work had managed to get his own way for a couple of years because fellow workers wanted to avoid any unpleasant confrontations. A new recruit stood up to him as well as reported his behavior to a senior manager. The bully was removed from the department.

2 AID UNDERSTANDING

Conflict can aid understanding between employees because it forces people to adopt a position and to justify their actions and beliefs. For example, a consultant was drafted into an insurance company to coach the sales team about new recruitment techniques. The majority of the team was not persuaded by the coaching, but his presence forced them to make a stand and explain why they thought their existing methods were generally better while admitting what changes they had to make.

3 PUSH FOR CHANGE

Conflict can encourage change by making people look at an old problem in a new light, potentially turning a difficulty into an opportunity. For example, a small food retailer that had operated in the same site for 30 years faced a major challenge when a leading supermarket chain opened a new shop opposite them. The retailer decided that instead of competing with them on everyday products, they would serve organic food products. This ensured their survival.

4 FOSTER TEAM SPIRIT

When a team experiences a dispute and manages to overcome all its differences, the team spirit is generally strengthened because it has faced a potentially damaging challenge but found a way of solving it to the satisfaction of the majority. For example, a team of eight people in a bank thought they had their fair share of interpersonal problems until a rival bank acquired their bank. Suddenly, they were faced with new management problems and the fear of losing their jobs if they didn't achieve certain targets. Confronting a common enemy—the unwanted new management—the team patched most of its former differences and worked together much more closely to produce good results.

defining conflict

Sources of conflict

WHO IN THE WORKPLACE CAN BE INVOLVED IN CONFLICT?

1 MANAGER AND EMPLOYEE
This type of conflict is more straightforward to settle because a manager, as the senior partner in a conflict, can resort to his higher position in the company hierarchy and impose the outcome on the subordinate.

2 MANAGER AND MANAGER
This type of conflict demands more tact from both participants because they can't resort to seniority or traditional lines of command to settle the dispute.

3 EMPLOYEE AND EMPLOYEE
This refers to all lower level employees who work together. In their disagreements, they can refer to a senior manager to act as a mediator in discussions.

HIGH-PROFILE WORKPLACE CONFLICTS

The most publicized types of conflict in the workplace, because they typically involve lawsuits and potential media coverage, are

1 Sexual harassment

2 Bullying

3 Age discrimination

4 Unfair or constructive dismissal

TWO MOST COMMON SOURCES OF WORKPLACE CONFLICTS
The two basic sources of conflict, described in more detail in the following section, are

1 SUBSTANTIVE CONFLICT
These conflicts involve disputes over facts, procedures, objectives, and values.

2 INTERPERSONAL CONFLICT
These involve basically a clash of personality types.

HOW TO DIFFERENTIATE?

It is vital to work out whether a conflict is caused by disagreement over concrete actions, decisions, and business ideas or whether it is the result of a personality clash. These are easy to get blurred but be honest about the sources of your anger. To help you define, try answering the following:

1 Do you get angry with the other party on a daily basis or only when particular work-related issues are raised?

2 When you are angry with the other party, are you sure you are not blowing it out of proportion? Would you feel the same if someone else shared the other party's viewpoint?

3 Are there any issues on which you agree with the other person?

defining conflict

Substantive conflict

There are many causes of substantive conflict. Generally the term refers to disputes arising from one or more of the following aspects of working life.

1 TASKS

People with differences in visions, quality expectations, and objectives have different approaches to handling everyday tasks. A person who likes to plan tasks out to every last detail will clash with a more impulsive worker who prefers to act spontaneously and rectify any details later in the day.

2 FACTS/DATA

When people have access to different information, there will inevitably be disagreement because they are working from a different set of figures. This type of dispute is generally easy to resolve because both parties can check their sources, discuss the reliability of the sources, and check how up-to-date their facts are.

3 GOALS/OBJECTIVES

In larger companies, mid or lower level employees will generally be working toward a set of objectives that has been prescribed by senior management. However, when managers are working together on a project with responsibility for setting goals themselves, disputes will arise if the objectives differ. Even in these cases, the company's overall goals should provide some kind of framework for discussion and ensure that any personal goals are compatible with the overall aims of the corporation.

Substantive conflict continued

4

PROCESSES/METHODS

Even when people agree on objectives, they may still have completely different ways of achieving goals. They may be influenced by their personality or be influenced by practices in a previous job. The potential for disagreement on "how do we achieve what we want?" may be considerable.

5

VALUES

Many companies expect their staff to follow a particular set of values. For instance, the values of a financial services company, with its emphasis on profits, are likely to be rather different from the values of a charity. To complicate matters, each individual brings his or her own set of values to the job, and this can present grounds for considerable conflict. Because values are tied up with deeply felt, sometimes religious beliefs, these kinds of disputes are less straightforward to resolve than other substantive conflicts.

PROS OF SUBSTANTIVE CONFLICT

Substantive conflict, when it can be kept under control, has several benefits.

1

When people force each other to look at a problem in a new light, they question the status quo and challenge themselves to find the most appropriate solution, not to follow blindly what has worked in the past. For eample, a well-established bookstore had managed to survive for decades on cursory customer service and haphazard layout of books mainly because they had no competition. Then with the advent of internet book sales as well as the arrival of sleekly presented bookstores in the same road, a manager was poached from a fast moving consumer goods company to shake up the bookstore's way of doing things. He advocated revamping the interior of the store, introducing a café, and improving customer service. His methods were met with a lot of opposition, but eventually, the manager managed to turn the dwindling sales around.

2

Brainstorming can lead to improved working practices and to positive change. For example, a team of six creatives (a mix of copywriters, artists, and graphic designers) at an advertising agency found themselves quarreling. However, when they gathered in a more official scenario like a board room under the supervision of an account director, they found that expressing their creative differences led to a stimulating discussion.

Interpersonal conflict

Interpersonal conflict refers to those disagreements based on clashing personality types. In general, there are two common features of interpersonal conflict. It is:

1 WIDESPREAD

Personality clashes are common and indeed unavoidable in all workplaces. Only when robots instead of humans carry out all aspects of office jobs will disagreements come to an end. In fact, business thrives on the spark caused by conflicting opinions and lively arguments. Differences and a certain amount of tension produce creative results. A business in which all people have similar personalities would not thrive.

2 SUBJECTIVE

Unlike substantive conflicts that can generally be resolved by examining the facts, interpersonal conflict can prove a far greater challenge because it deals more with opinions than facts. There is no such thing as a better type of personality, only a different type. A person who thrives on doing things at the last minute will get impatient with the person who wants everything ordered, measured, and carried out in a timely fashion, and vice versa.

defining conflict

Categorizing personality types

There is no one correct way of identifying personality types. The following section offers just a few of the different ways of categorizing types of people.

USING "HEALTH" TERMS

1

CHOLERIC
These are strong personalities who are aggressive and bossy at work.

2

PHLEGMATIC
These people show little emotion, preferring to use logic over emotion to resolve problems.

3

SANGUINE
These people are generally optimistic and enthusiastic in nature. They tend to say "yes" without considering if they can follow through.

4

MELANCHOLIC
These are the deep thinkers within the company; they are obsessed with details and organization.

USING "MANAGEMENT" TERMS

1 PROBLEM SOLVER
This person thrives on negotiating to reach a satisfactory solution.

2 SUPER HELPER
This person loves to put others first but may be less able to analyze his own problems.

3 POWER BROKER
This person is focused on finding a practical solution with limited regard for the impact of a decision on personal relations.

4 FACILITATOR
This person can adapt easily to a range of different scenarios, allowing him or her to press for compromise in a group of fiercely competing factions.

5 FEARFUL LOSER
This worrier shies away from a conflict that will expose him or her.

Categorizing personality types continued

FOUR BASIC PERSONALITY TYPES

One of the most common categorizations of personality types in business today is known as the Myers-Briggs Type Indicator, based on psychological types described by the philosopher Carl Jung.

FAVORITE WORLD

Do you prefer to focus on the outer world or on your own inner world?

1
- If you are energized by other people and taking swift action.
- If you think out loud and need to bounce ideas off other people.
- If you don't work well on your own.

= You are an EXTROVERT.

2
- If you get your energy from your own thoughts and ideas.
- If you take a back seat in large meetings and prefer to listen rather than talk.
- If you work better when you have some quiet periods on your own.

= You are an INTROVERT.

AN EXAMPLE OF POTENTIAL CLASH

An extrovert will jump to conclusions without asking the introvert for his opinion, hurting his feelings and, more significantly, making a decision without looking at the facts. Conversely, at a meeting, the introvert's reluctance to speak up may cost the team a valuable chance to raise its profile.

Categorizing personality types continued

INFORMATION
Do you prefer to focus on the basic information you take in or do you prefer
to interpret and add meaning?

3
- If you prefer to use your five senses to gather information.
- If you prefer facts and details to interpretations.
- If you like to learn through sequential facts.

= You are a SENSOR.

4
- If you like looking at the big picture.
- If you get bored by small details.
- If you like looking at the possibilities and meanings behind the facts.

= You are INTUITIVE.

AN EXAMPLE OF POTENTIAL CLASH

A sensor may get upset that a meeting, scheduled to last an hour, spills over into two. The intuitive person, who is less worried about time, may be unaware of how a meeting overrunning may affect other parts of the business.

Categorizing personality types continued

DECISIONS

When making decisions, do you prefer to first look at logic and consistency or do you look first at the people and special circumstances?

5

- If you base your decisions on objective values.
- If you are described as logical, detached, and analytical.
- If you prefer to do what is right rather than what makes people happy.

= You are a THINKER.

6

- If you tend to make decisions based on what you believe will create harmony.
- If you like to accommodate the needs of others in order to avoid conflict.
- If you are good at putting yourself in others' shoes and consider other people's feelings before making a decision.

= You are a FEELER.

AN EXAMPLE OF POTENTIAL CLASH

If a thinker and a feeler work together as a team they could drive each other crazy by their different approaches to a simple task such as scheduling the day's events. A thinker will want to prioritize the most important tasks, while the feeler is much happier putting off the more unpleasant tasks and focusing on the most enjoyable activities, regardless of their importance.

Categorizing personality types continued

STRUCTURE
When dealing with the outside world, do you prefer to get things decided or do you prefer to stay open to new information and options?

7
- If you like making lists.
- If you are punctual and like order.
- If you like planning every detail of the day and get upset when plans unravel.

= You are a JUDGER.

Note that this does not necessarily mean that you are Judgmental.

8
- If you rely on spontaneous, creative ideas to get you through the day.
- If you tend to leave things to the last minute to create urgency and focus.
- If you like to turn work into play.

= You are a PERCEIVER.

AN EXAMPLE OF POTENTIAL CLASH

A judger likes to finish work on time, sometimes regardless of whether in fact the best possible job has been done. A perceiver is far more likely to approach work more openly and creatively and to spend considerable amounts of time in finding the best possible solution as opposed to being over-concerned about completing and handing the work in on time.

Situational sources of conflict

Aside from the potential personality conflicts latent in any workplace, there are certain situations or scenarios that are commonly sources of dispute. They include:

1 PRIORITIES
When people put their work first (typically, "this is the most urgent task right now, you have to help me") above everyone else's, you can guarantee conflict will ensue.

2 LIMITED RESOURCES
When there are too many people fighting over limited resources, particularly desk space, material, supplies, and equipments, conflict is inevitable.

3 CONFLICT OF INTEREST
When individuals are too busy fighting to achieve their own
goals and these goals differ from both other people's goals
and the company's goals, then disputes will arise.

4 CULTURE, RACE, ETHNICITY
People's ways of perceiving the world are shaped to a large
extent by their cultural backgrounds, race, and ethnicity.
People from distinctly different racial and cultural
backgrounds can experience some clashes, especially in
the initial stages before each side has made the effort to
understand the other.

Situational sources of conflict continued

5 GENDER, SEXUALITY
The way men and women have been taught to perceive
situations differently (the debate whether this is genetic or
taught is in itself an issue of conflict) can be seen as a source
for disagreement. The stereotype is that many men are more
focused on facts and problem solving while women put a
greater emphasis on emotional content of disputes and care
more about the impact of decisions on people.

6 KNOWLEDGE, EXPERIENCE
The relative experience of a worker in facing a problem will
also affect the way a conflict occurs. Individuals with little
experience in the workplace may react more emotionally to a
dispute as they don't have the resources to negotiate and they
may feel more threatened by the outcome as they can't
imagine what the outcome could be.

7 AGE

Studies show that intergenerational conflict may be replacing race, culture, and gender as the most potentially divisive situational source of conflict. This is the result of the different values shared by the baby boomer generation, typically at the senior management end of companies and the young generation of recent graduates. The new generation has far less interest in the corporate system, in a lifetime career, and in company loyalty. Most significantly, they don't tend to see their job as the main source of their well-being which is considerably different from the older generation's attitude.

8 MISCOMMUNICATION

The lack of communication about any company plans, initiatives, or new recruitments can cause major tension in an office environment, especially when rumors and accusations start flying.

defining conflict

Team conflict

A team environment presents one of the most common situational sources of conflict in the workplace.

WHAT TEAM ACTIVITIES CAN RESULT IN CONFLICT?

1

DECISION MAKING
This has the potential to be a major source of contention particularly in those teams where everyone has a voice and all are encouraged to have a say.

2

TEAM PROCEDURES
Establishing how a team works together, who makes up the rules, who is allowed to challenge the rules, who decides how the team operates, who sets up schedules, and other such matters can yield many day-to-day problems.

3 ADMINISTRATIVE MATTERS
Issues like resources, availability of computers, a budget, complaints procedures, and so on, are all potentially problematic for teams.

4 PROMOTIONS
Promoting a member of staff from team player to team leader can cause problems, if not handled with sensitivity by all concerned parties.

46

Team conflict continued

WHAT TEAM BEHAVIOR CAN CAUSE CONFLICT?

1 VETO
Even when there is no veto system in a team's rules book, if one member of a team makes a major stand against a generally accepted principle and continues to voice disapproval, there is potential trouble ahead if the other members don't persuade the dissenting team member to accept the team decision graciously.

2 DISREGARD FOR RULES
When a team member deviates from the generally accepted rules that the rest of the team follows and then fails to explain or appear to care about the impact on the rest of the team, there is room for dispute.

3 AUTHORITARIAN LEADER
When a team leader is anxious to exert authority in a small team that prefers to act through consensus, there are likely disputes on the horizon.

4 STRONG FRIENDSHIP
When two people have a particularly strong friendship in a small team (up to about eight people), there are both positive and negative repercussions:

- PRO: If the two members communicate together a lot, they can create a sociable feel that draws other members to opening up about beliefs and aspirations. It may also make the group more enjoyable to work in.

- CON: When two members of staff are too close together, others can feel isolated. The team may split up into smaller sections, which can cause disunity and people taking sides during key decision moments.

Key questions: What is conflict?

1 WHAT COMPONENTS CREATE CONFLICT?
- NUMBERS: The presence of two or more forces.
- DIFFERENCES: The forces have a different set of beliefs, actions, and objectives.
- DESIRE TO WIN: Both sides want to win without compromising their goals.
- CLOSE PROXIMITY: Both sides are forced to interact with each other regularly.

2 WHAT ARE THE TWO BIGGEST MYTHS ABOUT CONFLICT?
- You can always avoid conflict at work. This is not true in the real world.
- Conflict is a bad thing. In fact, conflict can bring several benefits.

3 WHO CAN GET INVOLVED IN A CONFLICT?
- Manager and employee
- Manager and manager
- Employee and employee

4

WHAT ARE THE MOST COMMON SOURCES OF CONFLICT?
- SUBSTANTIVE: Disputes over facts, procedures, objectives, and values.
- INTERPERSONAL: A clash of personality types.

5

CAN YOU DESCRIBE BASIC PERSONALITY TYPES?
- Extroavert
- Introvert
- Sensor
- Intuitive
- Thinker
- Feeler
- Judger
- Perceiver

6

WHAT ARE COMMON SITUATIONAL SOURCES OF CONFLICT
- Priorities
- Limited resources
- Conflict of interest
- Culture, race, ethnicity
- Gender, sexuality
- Knowledge, experience
- Age
- Miscommunication

7

WHAT ARE THE COMMON TYPES OF TEAM CONFLICT?
- TEAM ACTIVITIES: decision making, procedures, administrative matters
- TEAM BEHAVIOR: veto, breaking rules, authoritarian leader, friendship

KEY QUESTIONS

2

the costs of conflict

The costs of conflict

THIS CHAPTER AIMS TO EXAMINE:

1 The most common reasons why managers choose to ignore the costs of conflict at work.

2 The direct costs of conflict at work.

3 The hidden costs of conflict at work.

4 The potential benefits of conflict at work.

WHY MANAGERS CHOOSE TO IGNORE THE COSTS OF CONFLICT

1

IGNORANCE
Many managers perceive that if they don't have to deal with
high-profile and self-evident conflicts such as unionized labor,
then disputes at work don't really affect their bottom line.
This ignores the many other direct and hidden costs of
conflict at work described in this chapter.

2

UNJUSTIFIABLE USE OF TIME
With managers trying to focus on core business, devoting
attention to conflict demands more time than they probably
feel they cannot justify either to their superiors or to the rest
of their workforce.

The costs of conflict continued

3 LACK OF RESPONSIBILITY

Traditionally, the costs of conflict resolution such as money spent on sexual harassments cases or unfair dismissals, have been the exception rather than the rule. Managers haven't been accountable for these costs so the time spent on this process has not been highly valued by the typical organization because it does not appear on financial statements. Shareholders and owners of companies have not required managers either to provide hidden costs of conflict. This may change in the future when companies can quantify the lost productivity and opportunity costs that on-going workplace conflict creates. Managers will expect to become involved in conflict and see conflict resolution as both a valuable and necessary part of leading a team.

4 MEASURING DIFFICULTIES

Measuring the direct and hidden costs of conflicts at work is not impossible but it is highly subjective and demands careful and painstaking attention. Most managers are loathe to inject extra energy into finding the appropriate personnel to quantify the cost of conflict. (They are most certainly averse to paying extra funds for the personnel too.) But a growing number of companies are becoming convinced that there are numerous financial gains from managing conflict successfully at work, both by preventing law suits and by freeing up more time for the core aspects of the business.

5 NEGATIVE PUBLICITY

Managers may also think that by lingering on studies about conflict at work, they are drawing attention to disputes that they don't necessarily want publicized to superiors. Shouldn't the managers be preventing these conflicts? Maybe it's better to lower their profile, is their line of argument.

Direct costs of conflict

There are certain direct costs of conflicts that do prove easier to quantify.

1

LEGAL FEES

The most obvious cost of workplace conflict are court cases, whether they revolve around most typically, unfair dismissals or more exceptionally, sexual harassment cases. Legal fees can be included in a company's operating expenses. It has been estimated that the 500 senior human resources executives in the United States spend almost a fifth of their time on activities related to litigation.

2

SEVERANCE PAY

Whether voluntary or involuntary, companies have to spend money on severance packages for disgruntled employees who may have been persuaded to remain in the company if an effective conflict resolution system had been in place.

3 RECRUITMENT COSTS OF NEW EMPLOYEES
The costs of recruiting (advertising the position in the media, spending time on the interviewing process, potential salary hikes to attract recruits) new employees who replace fired ones can be considerable.

4 TRAINING, DEVELOPMENT COSTS OF NEW EMPLOYEES
Whereas people who left the company have often been there a significant time and required little additional training, new recruits demand specialized training at a cost. The manager does not even have any guarantee he will be able to retain the new employees.

Direct costs of conflict continued

5 THEFT/SABOTAGE

Much of employee theft in a company, whether it be petty theft involving photocopy paper to more serious fiddling of expense accounts, stems from a disloyal, hostile attitude to the company. When it comes to sabotage, employees must have been deeply angered into taking aggressive action. Typical sabotage can include

- Hacking into computer programs

- Damaging computers, software, and other pieces of office equipment.

Theft can include

- Taking basic office supplies (like stationery) home

- Stealing expensive equipment

6 MISSED DEADLINES/LATE DELIVERIES

■ Conflicts can lead to individuals and teams missing deadlines. This in turn leads to unhappy customers and potential penalties for late deliveries.

■ Conflicts can affect the quality of work, and this can prove costly if managers have to devote extra time to redoing work, employing extra staff to meet revised deadlines, or buying new supplies so that goods can be produced for a second time.

Hidden costs of conflict

Aside from the more visible costs of conflict normally played out in courtrooms, there are numerous side effects to conflicts that are harder to quantify but just as damaging. These include the following:

1

LOWERED JOB MOTIVATION
When people work with others whom they perceive as "problem" colleagues, there can be a direct impact on performance caused by a loss of motivation and increased stress trying to avoid conflict or handling the conflict unsatisfactorily. A prolonged conflict reflects poorly on senior management, creating a further loss of trust and faith.

2

ADDITIONAL WORK BURDEN
Staff turnover is not only costly in terms of recruitment costs. It also has an indirect impact on general performance in the department which has to adjust to the loss of a worker. Many employees, even those who are relieved to see their former colleague depart the company, may have to take on additional roles until a new hiring is made. It is difficult to assess the exact impact on the bottom line without measuring productivity on a monthly basis and making comparisons for months when the status quo is maintained and other months when major staff changes occur.

3

ABSENTEEISM

Stress and anger toward co-workers can be handled by some workers by simply staying away from the workplace for chunks of time. The U.S. absenteeism rate in 2006 is forecast to reach 2.5 percent, the highest since 1999 when it was 2.7 percent according to a survey conducted by the Harris Interactive consulting firm. It was found that personal illness accounted for 35 percent of unscheduled absences, while personal needs made up 18 percent and stress 12 percent. The three factors could be linked directly to stress in the workplace. The survey also revealed that absenteeism costs some large employers an estimated $850,000 per year in direct payroll costs.

The loss to productivity is not only felt in the absent individual's work, for instance missed appointments and deadlines, but in the work of colleagues who remain in the office, forced to take on extra duties, and becoming disgruntled with absent workers.

Hidden costs of conflict continued

4 LACK OF FOCUS, COMMITMENT

Unhappy staff don't just stop producing work to the best of their ability. They lose commitment and focus instead on finding a new job. Looking for alternative employment and following through with applications, can take up a considerable amount of time from the ordinary working day.

5 DISTRACTED MANAGEMENT

A senior manager spends an increasing amount of time trying to resolve conflict, particularly given the continuing trend for downsizing. While managers are expected to oversee employees, if they don't have the tools to handle disputes, they will lose valuable time that they could have used on core aspects of their work, not just the daily operational tasks but more strategic and creative thinking time.

6

HEALTH COSTS

Some absences from the workplace are legitimately due to injuries and illnesses. In the case of sickness, there are studies illustrating how stress in the workplace can bring on illnesses because defense mechanisms are lowered. Companies are struggling with huge annual increases in health insurance premiums and healthcare costs. These medical costs can consume half of corporate profits for many companies, according to the Wellness Councils of America, a leading resource for worksite wellness. As a result, more than 81 percent of American businesses with 50 or more employees today invest in some form of health promotion program including stop-smoking classes, promotions to exercise more, and stress management.

For instance, one well-known multinational company, Johnson and Johnson, was reported to have reduced its absenteeism rate by 15 percent within two years of introducing a wellness program. The company also cut its hospital costs by 34 percent over three years

Hidden costs of conflict continued

7 COMPANY REPUTATION
Business disputes that end up in court garner much unwanted publicity, and for companies that sell products or services, this is generally bad publicity. The impact is twofold: on customers who may question the image of the company, especially in today's business climate where companies are competing over ethical standards and their sense of corporate responsibility. It can also damage recruitment as high-caliber candidates are driven away from applying for jobs.

8 MISSED OPPORTUNITIES
The costs of missing key business opportunities may seem difficult to quantify. If a company didn't take a particular course, how can one deduce missed benefits ? Sometimes, it is sufficient to analyze key competitors and see what they have gained from a shrewd business move. For instance, the competitor may have bought a smaller company or carved a new niche in the market. These are actions that your company could also have taken but failed to pursue because it spent too much time on internal conflict. If the competitor is successful with its acquisition or market opening, this will be reflected in increased sales or higher revenue in six months to a year's time. These are quantifiable gains.

9 TRAINING TIME

Certainly, training time is essential and valuable for new employees. However, when a manager has to spend too much time training as a result of a flurry of new hires—partly caused by people leaving the company due to workplace conflict— this can be costly to the company. For instance, when a new employee joins a team, it may take some time before the person becomes a productive member. It may also take some time to gauge how well the new recruit fits in with the rest of the team. Other team members may under perform while they devote time to extra training.

10 DECISION MAKING

Adequate gathering of information is essential to making a decision, and this process will be weakened by poor communication among staff. Decisions based on key facts and thoroughly calculated outcomes are also likely to be contaminated by power struggles. Conflict can even cause some staff to hold on to key pieces of information in a "knowledge is power" scenario that can have an impact on effective decision making.

Potential benefits of conflict

Although this section has underlined the direct and hidden costs of conflict, it is vital to stress that conflict can also, when adequately handled, yield substantial benefits,

1 FOSTERS GROWTH

There is little doubt that growth can by stymied by protracted workplace conflict. But growth can also be bolstered by conflict when it forces managers to make difficult decisions that would otherwise have been postponed. These decisions might include

■ Acquiring a new company

■ Launching a new product

■ Letting staff go

■ Actively expanding into new sectors

Such decisions will hopefully lead to business growth. In these circumstances, conflict is vital to prevent a company from becoming stagnant.

2

PROMOTES UNDERSTANDING

People's positions and ideals can remain hidden in a company or department where there is apparent harmony. However, a proper understanding of everyone's motives and goals is essential for adequate decision making and the mapping out of strategies. Conflict forces people to stake their claim in the business and, if resolved properly, can lead to improved understanding of the company's future direction and people's aspirations within the company.

Potential benefits of conflict continued

3 CHALLENGES STATUS QUO

Even though all companies require the majority of employees to be in agreement with general policies because otherwise there would be disorder, the most successful companies invariably have members who are not afraid to challenge the status quo. Providing alternative viewpoints and asking awkward questions can be seen as causing unnecessary conflict, but it is in fact vital to question the direction of the company and to test that its underlying assumptions continue to be valid.

4 PROMOTES CREATIVITY

When two or more parties in a company are stuck in a seemingly stalemate situation where no member will budge, it requires a considerable degree of creativity by managers to think of a solution that will enable all parties to overcome their differences.

5 IMPROVES PERSONAL SKILLS
Interpersonal skills such as effective listening, mutual understanding, and the appreciation of different viewpoints can only be improved by putting them into practice. With its potential for damage to the business, interpersonal conflict provides the opportunity to put these interpersonal skills to the test and to improve overall performance.

6 BOOSTS COMPETITIVE TEETH
Because conflict is literally the competition of interests, it represents an opportunity to hone the workforce's sense of competition which is key to creating a distinctive edge from the competition. Competition in your sector, in any form, can be beneficial in the longer term.

Key questions: The costs

1 WHY DO MANAGERS CHOSE TO IGNORE THE COSTS OF CONFLICT?
- ■ IGNORANCE. They ignore the direct and hidden costs of every day conflict at work.
- ■ LACK OF RESPONSIBILITY. Managers fail to see they are accountable for conflict at work.
- ■ DIFFICULT TO QUANTIFY. Managers find it difficult to quantify exactly how conflict affects the bottom line.
- ■ UNJUSTIFIABLE USE OF TIME. Busy managers tend to put conflict at work on the back burner.

2 WHAT ARE THE DIRECT COSTS OF CONFLICT?
- ■ LEGAL FEES. Litigation usually revolves around unfair dismissals, more rarely, sexual harassment.
- ■ SEVERANCE PAY/RECRUITMENT COSTS. Companies have to fork out severance packages for disgruntled employees and spend extra money on training new recruits.
- ■ THEFT/SABOTAGE. Frustrated employees can steal equipment, fiddle expenses, and hack into computer programs.
- ■ MISSED DEADLINES. Individuals embroiled in conflict are more likely to deliver work late.

3 WHAT ARE THE HIDDEN COSTS OF CONFLICT?

- LOWERED JOB MOTIVATION. Unhappy staff lose motivation and commitment and focus instead on finding a new job.
- ADDITIONAL WORK BURDEN. Staff turnover creates extra work.
- ABSENTEEISM. Overburdened staff tend to take more days off sick.
- DISTRACTED MANAGEMENT. Managers have less time for strategy.

4 WHAT ARE THE POTENTIAL BENEFITS OF CONFLICT?

- FOSTERS GROWTH. Conflict can force managers to make difficult decisions that may lead to growth.
- PROMOTES UNDERSTANDING. Conflict encourages people to stake their claim in the business and understand the company's direction.
- CHALLENGES STATUS QUO. People with alternative view points help to test that the company's assumptions continue to be valid.
- PROMOTES CREATIVITY. Problems encourage creative solutions that will enable all parties to overcome their differences.
- BOOSTS COMPETITIVE TEETH.

KEY QUESTIONS

3

avoiding conflict

Anticipating conflict

This chapter outlines strategies to help you avoid the negative consequences of conflict at the workplace. It looks at

1 How to anticipate "conflicting" scenarios

2 How to anticipate "conflicting" behavior

3 How to train staff to manage conflict

4 How to foster team spirit

5 How to motivate employees

HOW TO ANTICIPATE "CONFLICTING" SCENARIOS

As a manager, you will inevitably face conflicts that emerge out of the blue. However, there are disputes that you can prepare yourself for, anticipate, and deflect before they break out. The following steps will help to sharpen your alertness to conflicting situations:

1

MAKE A NOTE OF "CONFLICT" TRENDS

Ask yourself if there is a pattern in the conflicts that have occurred at your workplace this year? Can you spot a pattern? If you haven't written them down, this is the time to start a diary. It could help you to chart the occurrences of these conflicts and to see if there are particular triggers to conflict. For instance, if you are in the retail market, does pressure double in the pre-Christmas period? Do you make alternative arrangements like hiring extra staff or providing incentives to staff in the form of bonuses or extra holidays after the busy season? Does the company have any records of recent disagreements and, if so, how were they handled?

Anticipating conflict continued

2 EXAMINE PROCESSES

Do you have an official set of rules of conduct at work that employees can follow? Do you expect employees to work out the company policy on disputes as they go along? If you don't have a system, why not consider creating one that establishes rules such as appointing a person whose function is to record any unhappy situations at work. This person would be responsible for setting up a meeting between the conflicting employees under supervision. If you think it sounds too official, consider that the alternative to providing a formal channel to air grievances is gossip and back biting in office bathrooms and photo copying rooms.

3 REVIEW HIRING POLICY
Have your most recent appointments (for instance in the last year) been successful? Have new hires fitted in to the company? If not, should you reconsider focusing more on behavioral interview questions during the hiring process?

4 EXAMINE PUNISHMENT/REWARD SYSTEM
When was the last time you asked staff if they think they are adequately recompensed for the work they carry out? This is not an excuse for them to demand higher salaries but to provide honest feedback on whether they feel the company does enough to recognize improvements in behavior and results. Also, ask about any instances of punishments or reprimands that they feel have been inadequately handled. If employees feel their concerns and development matter to the management, there is less chance of resentment and a sense of injustice—which leads to conflict—building up.

Anticipating conflicting behavior

Managers need to be alert to signs of conflict between colleagues so they can be proactive in reducing the chances of disputes blowing out of proportion. These are some ways to heighten your awareness of potential conflicts:

1 **LEARN TO READ TYPICAL SIGNS**
The following are normal signs of a conflict at work:

- Normally amiable colleagues who don't speak to each other or actively ignore each other

- Colleagues who bad mouth one another

- Colleagues who refuse to co-operate with each other

- Office teams that used to work united but are now divided into cliques

2 BE ALERT TO PERIODS OF CHANGE IN THE COMPANY.

Periods of change are notoriously difficult to handle in a company. Changes can come from various sources including a major restructuring following an acquisition or merger, an office move, the launch of a new product or service, or the departure of key team members. These are some of the most common effects of change:

■ FEAR

More often than not, normally reasonable people can tend to become difficult when confronted with an end to old routines, even when these were disliked. Expect people to cause a fuss during periods of change.

■ CONFUSION

When a period of change is either poorly communicated to staff or badly anticipated, the outcome is confusion. In the absence of information, the rumor mill takes over, adding the fuel of speculation to the reigning confusion. Some people may feel their share of responsibilities and workload increase and feel incapable of handling the extra work. Others feel underutilized and lack motivation to push themselves at work.

Anticipating fear and confusion

These are tips to avoid the negative effects of change and confusion.

1 Never forget the emotional responses people go through during a time of upheaval and possible job losses.

2 Inform people as much as possible as to the changes, dispel rumors, and let them understand why things are changing and what it means for them.

3 Give people plenty of notice of proposed changes, but do not divulge half-formed plans. Make sure you are clear about what is going to happen.

4 LIsten to their anxieties; be understanding and supportive.

5 Don't underestimate how even the most trivial changes in an office can affect morale.

6 If at all possible, make sure everyone hears the news at the same time.

Coping with hostility

Managers are able to cope better with conflict if they have a better understanding and knowledge of what makes people react with hostility in the workplace. These are some issues to consider:

1 FOCUS ON BEHAVIOR, NOT PEOPLE
Labeling a person as difficult is an easy trap to fall into. The danger is that there is hardly a general consensus within a company as to who is a troublesome person. It depends whether you are in the receiving end of your particular problem colleague, boss, or employee or not. That's why it's more useful to talk about difficult behavior than difficult people. This prevents any criticism of behavior from being perceived as a personal or biased attack. Focusing on particular instances of difficult behavior also allows the people involved in the conflict, as well as any observers, to take a more objective look at a situation.

2 BE AWARE OF DIFFERENCES

The very diversity of perspectives and working styles that are inevitably present in a working team are most frequently the source of conflict, which participants describe as "difficult behavior." In many cases, a manager's definition of a difficult person is an individual whose work style is different from her own. If you are having a problem with someone at work, try to answer these questions honestly to see whether your own prejudices are coloring your attitude to the person:

■ Does a pattern exist for you in your interaction with co-workers? Do you recognize that you have hot buttons that are easily pushed?

■ Is the difficult person always behaving badly or are they just having a bad day?

■ Are you sure you're not reacting negatively to practically everything they do because something about their appearance (for instance, hair, moustache, perfume, mannerisms) remind you of an unpleasant person in your past?

Coping with hostility continued

3 UNDERSTAND DIFFERENT PRIORITIES
In addition to different behavior patterns, workers have diverging goals and motivations. The three most common priorities are:

■ GETTING A JOB DONE
Deadlines are necessary in most businesses but especially in the media, publishing, and retail worlds where swift access to information or goods is essential. Urgent action demands a direct, decisive hands-on approach.

■ DOING A JOB RIGHT
Most people strive to do a good job but sometimes the effort to provide a speedy service will mean sacrificing total accuracy, careful analysis, and elaborate planning. But for perfectionists and sticklers for detail, getting the job right is the ultimate goal, and these people dislike being pressurized by time demands.

■ GETTING ALONG WITH PEOPLE
Relating well to people is key to service and tourism industries. Companies whose goal is to provide either a swift or highly valued service may prove alienating for people whose main commitment is to provide friendly customer service or to operate within a friendly, open environment.

CASE STUDY

Take the example of three managers (John, Clare, and Tim) of a specialist travel agency that provides tailor-made holiday breaks for executives.

GETTING A JOB DONE

John likes to plunge into assignments. He loves getting immediate results. That's what makes him tick at work. He likes ending the day, knowing he has managed to sell a certain number of travel packages. If there is a deadline, he wants to meet it, tick his list, and move on. John doesn't dwell on missed opportunities.

DOING A JOB RIGHT

Clare loves to select the best possible travel solution for her clients. She thrives on matching clients' needs with a particular destination. She's rather a stickler for facts and details. Her approach means she will take rather a long time to close a "trip" deal with customers.

GETTING ALONG WITH PEOPLE

Tim loves interacting with people, with both his colleagues and his customers. He believes passionately that providing a friendly, helpful service is the most important aspect of his job. Although providing a suitable travel package or destination is important, he believes customers are ultimately persuaded by excellent customer service.

Training to manage conflict

Training staff to resolve their own conflict is an ambitious task but could yield rewarding results. These are some recommendations:

1 ENCOURAGE STAFF TO EMBRACE CONFLICT

This sounds like a contradiction, but it isn't. Of course, conflict can be negative if not handled properly, but it is also useful in solving problems. It's healthy for people to disagree with each other and to lobby for different ideas. Let them know this by practicing what you preach and asking them to express their opinion before you speak your own. Tell staff that you want to hear of any disagreements and differing opinions. That way, you train staff to confront conflict, rather than shying away from it or denying that it exists. Don't forget to thank people who are willing to take a stand. Strong opinions, eloquently expressed and lobbied for by those who hold them, are likely to be the lifeblood of your organization.

2 ARRANGE A MEETING TO AIR DIFFERENCES

Having let staff know that you appreciate the airing of opinions, follow this up by arranging an actual meeting where they can put this into practice. Explain at the beginning of the meeting that this is serving several purposes:

■ It provides an opportunity to make their opinions heard.

■ It serves as training on how to conduct such gatherings.

■ It serves as a model for future similar sessions, when you might not be present.

Training to manage conflict continued

3 ESTABLISH GROUND RULES FOR MEETINGS
At the meeting, establish ground rules for conducting these kinds of meetings. These rules will help to establish boundaries for airing disagreements in a constructive manner even when you are not around. In fact, you are seeking to get them to apply these rules independently of you so they learn to sort out any preliminary sources of conflict themselves. Examples of ground rules are

■ One person will be appointed to chair the meeting.

■ Another person will take down notes.

■ There will be no use of abusive language or swear words.

■ There will be no derogatory comments or personal attacks.

■ Everyone will have an allotted time (no more than five minutes) to air an opinion.

■ During a speech, people will listen and not interrupt.

■ People should keep discussions to issues, not personalities.

4 PROVIDE FRAMEWORK FOR ONE-ON-ONE SESSIONS

Not all disagreements will be conducted in the safe environment of a meeting with other people acting as potential buffers. Sometimes, two people will meet to discuss their problems in private (or sometimes in public if emotions are running high). Without a mediator, they might find it useful to remember the following guidelines:

■ Both parties should find a mutually convenient time to discuss their problem.

■ They must arrange not to be interrupted at all during their exchange.

■ They should remember the basic principles of listening, which are to paraphrase (to repeat back to the speaker what he or she has said in his or her own words), and to reframe (which is to change the focus of a negative statement). For instance, if one person says, "I feel you never take my ideas into account," the other person should try to rephrase the statement in a more positive light like "I understand that you would like your views to be taken seriously and discussed by the team."

How to foster team spirit

Creating a closely knit team not only makes it more efficient but also reduces considerably the opportunity for conflict. These are some recommended steps to encourage team spirit.

1

CREATE A SHARED VISION/GOAL
Divided objectives are one of the central sources of conflict so establishing some common goals is one of the first steps in helping team members to feel part of something larger than each individual. The main driving force for this feeling of unity is for the company or team leader to define an objective. The goal needs to be specific, realistic, and easily measured. For instance: "to raise sales by 50 percent within three months" or "to win another 5,000 customers by the end of the year."

2

DEFINE EXPECTATIONS
The team leader should also underline what he expects each member to accomplish individually to help achieve the desired results. That way each person is motivated to fulfill his or her part in the overall team effort.

3 UNDERSTAND ROLE OF TEAM
Team members should be told why the team has been
created, what function it plays within the company, and what
similar teams have accomplished in the past.

4 INSTILL CONFIDENCE
The team will also work much more effectively if the manager
is able to explain:

■ The qualities that made him choose the team members

■ How he expects to recognize their contributions (by offering
promotions or bonuses, for instance)

■ The skills team members expect to grow and develop while
working in the team.

How to foster team spirit continued

5 ESTABLISH ACCOUNTABILITY
Team members feel much more responsible for their actions if they are given accountability for the team's achievements. For instance, will team members face reprisals if they don't achieve their targets? Will the company management offer any rewards?

6 COMMUNICATE IMPORTANT FACTS
The sharing of information is vital to sustain a shared vision, and a manager is advised to keep all members up to date with current issues through email alerts and memos. The information provided should be brief and simple. Messages should have a particular point such as "sales figures" or "staff changes." Team members don't want to be bogged down with irrelevant details. That will only encourage dissent, which you are trying to avoid.

7 PRAISE EFFORTS
A team likes to have its efforts acknowledged, even when it is going through difficult times, which may not be their fault but the result of a difficult business environment or other external factors. A manager needs to let the team know when they are doing a good job.

8 LAY DOWN GRIEVANCE PROCEDURES
In spite of all the above efforts, preventing a conflict within a team is not always possible. When it occurs, make sure you have a formal procedure that can be followed so that aggrieved workers know who to file a complaint with and what procedures (meetings, mediation) will be followed.

avoiding conflict
Motivating individuals

One of the main causes for conflict in the workplace is when managers fail
to motivate their workforce adequately, which leads to employees feeling
dissatisfied and underappreciated. These are some general tips for
motivating employees.

1 KEEP NEGATIVES DOWN
Steer away from negative statements unless they have really
done something wrong. If there is room for improvement, let
them know first where they have achieved their targets and
suggest ways in which they can improve on those. Some
people, once branded as ineffective, lose so much self-
confidence and goodwill that they justify future negative
criticism of their work.

2 DON'T BE AFRAID TO COMPLIMENT
Credit them for good work done. Be specific with your
compliments. The employees will be pleased that you have
noticed and will continue trying. When goals have been met,
shift the goal posts to bolster ambition. This works best for
the more productive workers. For the slower employees, be
realistic about their rate of improvement.

3 PROVIDE BENEFICIAL TRAINING
Encourage employees to seek the training they think will
most benefit them and their jobs. Make sure that the keen
candidates are not the only ones who attend training sessions.
The more self-effacing employees would also benefit from
external input.

4 GIVE INCENTIVES
Provide financial incentives if certain targets are met.
However, you might want to be discreet about bonuses as it
might discourage those workers who fail to receive any bonus
at all. A bonus that can be shared by an entire department, for
instance, may be fairer than singling out an individual, unless
your company operates a regular "salesman of the month" or
similar scheme.

Motivation during change

Forgetting to motivate staff during periods of change can encourage conflict. Managers should be aware that there are typically, three phases during a period of change.

1 RESISTANCE
Employees, even those who disliked the old system, oppose the breaking of old habits, which are perceived of as "safe" or "comfortable." They may fear a change in the hierarchy within the department or that any new systems will place extra demands on their working day.

2 RE-EDUCATION
Employees may not be aware that they are learning a new method of working because they are too busy resisting it. Effective communication and training will gradually bring the workforce around to implementing new ways.

3 ACCEPTANCE

Once the new system is operating satisfactorily, employees will hopefully be doing their best to fit in with the new system, particularly if the manager has communicated the cons of the old system and the pros of the new one. Once the system has been in place for a few months, inform staff of tangible improvements that have resulted from the new system, for example:

■ We are fulfilling orders on average two days faster than under the old system.

■ We are on target to increase profits by 5 percent by the end of the year.

Key questions: Avoiding conflict

1 HOW CAN YOU ANTICIPATE CONFLICTING SCENARIOS?

■ TRACK "CONFLICT" TRENDS. Start a diary and try to identify a pattern in the conflicts that have occurred at your workplace this year. Underline the main triggers.

■ EXAMINE PROCESSES. Create an official set of rules of conduct at work that employees can follow.

■ REVIEW HIRING POLICY. Reconsider focusing more on behavioral interview questions during the hiring process?

■ EXAMINE PUNISHMENT/REWARD SYSTEM. Do you give staff honest feedback, praise and incentives to encourage future good work?

2 HOW CAN YOU TRAIN STAFF TO MANAGE CONFLICT?

■ ENCOURAGE STAFF TO EMBRACE CONFLICT. Let staff know that it's healthy for people to disagree and to lobby for different ideas. Train staff to confront conflict, not shy away or deny that it exists.

■ ARRANGE A MEETING TO AIR DIFFERENCES. If people need to discuss problems, arrange a meeting where you can monitor a dispute and let people air their opinions. Establish boundaries for airing disagreements in a constructive manner if you are not there.

■ PROVIDE FRAMEWORK FOR ONE-TO-ONE SESSIONS. Sometimes, two people will meet to discuss their problems in private. Make guidelines clear such as fixing a mutually convenient time and to allow no interruptions.

3

HOW DO YOU FOSTER TEAM SPIRIT?

■ CREATE A SHARED VISION/GOAL. Establish some common goals to help team members feel part of something larger than each individual.

■ DEFINE EXPECTATIONS. The team leader should also underline what he expects each member to accomplish individually to help achieve the desired results.

■ ESTABLISH ACCOUNTABILITY. Team members feel much more responsible for their actions if they are given accountability for the team's achievements.

4

HOW DO YOU MOTIVATE INDIVIDUALS?

■ KEEP NEGATIVES DOWN. Steer away from negative statements unless they have really done something wrong.

■ REMEMBER TO PRAISE. Credit them for good work done. Be specific with your compliments. The employee will be pleased that you have noticed any progress.

■ PROVIDE BENEFICIAL TRAINING. Encourage employees to seek the training they think will most benefit them and their jobs.

■ GIVE INCENTIVES. Provide financial incentives if certain targets are met or exceeded.

4

barriers to conflict resolution

barriers to conflict resolution

Denial and avoidance

This chapter looks at some of the most common obstacles to conflict resolution, usually sparked off by common responses to the existence of conflict at work. These are:

1. denial or avoidance
2. aggression
3. accommodation
4. compromise

We will look at each of these in turn.

DENIAL/AVOIDANCE

One of the biggest barriers to resolving a conflict is to deny that the conflict even exists, or if you do recognize it, you avoid doing anything about it, hoping the problem will somehow evaporate. For instance, in an advertising agency, an experienced copywriter tends to produce high-quality work but is often aggressive when she meets with clients, mainly major advertisers who are the agency's key clients. The account manager of the advertising agency—who is typically the interface between the ad agency and the client—may be aware that the copywriter's attitude to clients is posing problems with the client, but he chooses to avoid tackling it.

SYMPTOMS OF DENIAL/AVOIDANCE

If the advertiser, in spite of being reasonably happy with the creative output of the agency, chooses to end the relationship with the agency, the account director may not inform other managers in the agency about the reasons for the fallout in the relationship. Not only does he fail to acknowledge to himself or others, why the account may have been lost, he continues to use the problematic copywriter with a new advertiser, hoping that the problem will go away next time. This is "avoidance of action" at its most dangerous because it is spreading the existing conflict to other parts of the business.

Denial and avoidance continued

REASONS FOR DENIAL/AVOIDANCE

1 FAILURE AS A MANAGER
The account director may fear that by acknowledging the conflict caused by the copywriter's hostile attitude to clients, he is drawing attention to his own shortcomings as a manager. Why, for instance, did he not draw attention to the copywriter before about her challenging behavior?

2 FEAR OF UPSETTING THE COPYWRITER
The copywriter may have been a valuable asset to the agency in the past, and may still produce quality work. To bring up an existing problem with her and management now will upset her and others.

3 DISLIKE OF CHANGE
The account director knows that by having to take action with the copywriter, leading perhaps to a highly possible dismissal or walkout, he is going to be forced to embark on a recruiting process. He may prefer the status quo to the unknown.

4 DELUSION
The account director may believe that the benefits of keeping the copywriter outweigh the disadvantages. At the same time, he convinces himself that the problem is, in fact, trivial.

5 PROCRASTINATION
The account director decides it is best to give the copywriter one more opportunity with clients before he is obliged to make a final judgment.

Aggression

Aggressive behavior is characterized by an "I win, you lose" mentality, which appears to resolve a conflict conclusively. However, the apparent closure is almost always superficial. If the aggressive person seeks to win an argument or a point at the expense of someone else, the aggrieved party is likely to respond with anger, resentment, resistance, and fear. None of these reactions can bode well for team spirit or future cooperation between team members. In effect, the conflict will continue, even if it takes longer to resurface again once the initial impact of the aggressive behavior has finished.

SYMPTOMS OF AGGRESSION

If the account director, spotting the tensions the copywriter is causing in client meetings, simply chooses to reprimand the copywriter, blaming her for her poor behavior and issuing an official warning without waiting for any explanation, that would be considered an aggressive act.

To such an unwarranted attack, the copywriter is likely to lash back in anger. The absence of any proper dialog is unlikely to diffuse the situation. In fact, the creative copywriter may respond negatively, behaving even more awkwardly in the next meeting with clients.

Reasons for aggression

1 CORPORATE CULTURE
The prevailing ethos in many large companies is to show swift action and resolution, encouraging managers to be aggressive and controlling. The manager has to win, and the other person has to lose.

2 SPECIFIC SCENARIOS THAT VALUE AGGRESSION
Sometimes, managers are specifically taken on by a company to do jobs that are widely considered unpleasant such as firing people. Diplomacy and bridge-building skills are not seen as essential in these cases. Even if the aggressive practices start affecting the workplace, the manager in question may have moved on so reprisals or a backlash are more difficult. The problem occurs when such aggressive styles are transferred to other parts of the business where a more consensual approach is required.

3 FEELINGS OF INFERIORITY
People who feel unhappy with themselves or feel inadequate about their work, think aggression will raise their self-esteem.

4 DEFENSE MECHANISM
When managers feel under particular threat, they may anticipate any perceived or real trouble by attacking the source instead of carefully thinking what measure would be most appropriate.

5 COMPENSATING FOR PASSIVE BEHAVIOR
It's not unusual for passive people who have taken on more work than they can handle by being too fearful of making a fuss or who have been on the receiving end of aggressive behavior to have a sudden outburst of anger. This often surprising display of aggressive behavior is frequently not directed at the original source of aggression but at other passive workers.

Accommodation

Accommodating behavior is, in many ways, the opposite of aggression. It involves giving in to other people's demands as a way of defusing a potential conflict. Subordinates are far more likely to be accommodating with managers who have the power and experience to impose their will. As with aggression, the effects of accommodation are, more often than not, short-lived. When people feel they have had the needs of others put before their own, they can end up feeling resentful, angry, and powerless. The underlying reasons for the initial conflict won't have gone away, they are only left simmering.

The next time the employee is asked to do something and is again accommodating, the initial anger and resentment return to the surface, and the vicious cycle continues.

SYMPTOMS OF ACCOMMODATING BEHAVIOR

In the case of the account director, if he chose to indulge the copywriter and forgive her for her rude behavior in front of clients because of the quality of her work, he would be accommodating her. He lives with the behavior because of the high quality work. This could make him feel resentful about the copywriter's insensitivity to his problem and also powerless in being able to do anything to change the behavior.

The next time the copywriter is rude in a meeting, he will be reminded of all those other similar occasions, which he has not commented on and knows he should have. The frustration can cause him to act in an aggressive manner.

Reasons for accommodation

1 THE WILL TO PLEASE
People who accommodate others think that by pleasing them and putting their needs first, they may be rewarded by having their needs eventually seen to. This pattern of behavior is very common among young children who are constantly told that if they do what their parents tell them to do, they will be rewarded with special attention. However, when this ingrained pattern is transferred to the workplace, the incentives for the employer to follow through her end of the bargain with the employee who is eager to please are far less.

2 FEAR OF REJECTION
Another consequence of behavior patterns learned during infancy is that bad behavior will be punished by rejection or less attention. People who desist from expressing their opinions or raising objections to new plans or projects are afraid of being rejected or of being branded a difficult team player. In the workplace, these are the people who resist expressing their opinions.

3

LACK OF CONFIDENCE
Low self-esteem can lead people to avoid the spotlight at
work. The upshot is that passive people will say little in
meetings, provide no feedback on projects that they are
involved in, and end up being overlooked for challenging or
interesting new tasks.

4

EXCESSIVE EMPATHY
Although it is appropriate to take other people's feelings into
consideration, empathy can lead people to assume too much
responsibility for other peoples' feelings if they get hurt.

5

POLITENESS
Some people tend to confuse speaking their minds about
a subject with rudeness. They think being regarded as
considerate will be more valued than raising a valid objection.

Compromise

Compromise involves two or more people making a series of tradeoffs to avoid the ongoing conflict. It demands finding the middle path, the "least worst" solution for all parties concerned. On the surface, it appears ideal for situations where both sides are willing to give and take a little. However, when people are busy trying to get the best possible deal for themselves, they don't necessarily understand the other side's needs. The compromise they come to may only be temporary because both sides can feel resentful about not having pushed hard enough or having gained too little. Although reaching an agreement saves time and money, if nobody is really happy with the deal, and all parties feel they are losers, the results are not going to be positive for anyone.

SYMPTOMS OF COMPROMISING BEHAVIOR

In the case of the account director, he may have decided to talk to the copywriter and agree to extend deadlines for future work in exchange for the copywriter keeping her opinions to herself during client meetings. The copywriter may have pushed hard for this concession. Ultimately, the account director will feel angry that he promised to change the working patterns of his copywriter to appease her because the copywriter will try to squeeze further demands in the future and she will still find it difficult to be discreet in meetings with clients. Compromising has not made resolving the core conflict any easier, and in fact it has taken part of the equation that was working well—the work done by the copywriter in the time allowed—and made it worse. There is now no incentive for the copywriter to improve her behavior in front of the company's clients.

Reasons for compromise

1 AN EASY LIFE
Most workers decide at some stage or another, that to concede on a few points with a fellow worker or employee about working conditions is worthwhile if it promises to relieve tensions in the office.

2 FAILURE TO NEGOTIATE
Any ongoing negotiations to extract the worker's exact demands or to enforce specific conditions have failed so the worker is forced to compromise.

3 SPEEDY SOLUTION
Sometimes, workers have to take the quickest way out. Coming to a solution, however imperfect, often seems far better than prolonging conflict unnecessarily.

4 THE LEAST WORST SOLUTION
Reaching a compromise doesn't always have to be regarded in a negative light. Some managers see it as a way of satisfying everyone's needs and desires, even if these are limited. It is preferable to aggression.

5 NO POWER
There are occasions when the other party you are trying to negotiate with simply has more power over you. They could be either a customer (who is almost always right) or a manager. In the end, you have limited options to negotiate.

6 SHIFTING GOAL POSTS
Pragmatic workers can perceive that some objectives have to be adjusted according to circumstances and that it is essentially best to remain flexible and achieve some gains than to risk losing everything.

Additional barriers

Four other common obstacles to conflict resolution include

1 POOR COMMUNICATION
Poor or inadequate information (sometimes misinformation) is the cause of many problems at work, not least to the creation of conflict or the persistence of an old problem. Conflict resolution remains elusive when

- People are not listening to each other and base their judgments on what they think the opposing side is saying, rather than on what they are actually saying.

- One person assumes that another's well-documented and well-known views on a subject have not changed in any way, so she does not listen when in fact the second party has changed his mind on an issue.

2 EMOTIONS

Losing control of emotions is another frequent barrier to conflict resolution. Emotions have an impact on conflict in three main ways.

■ It is easy for emotions like anger, fear, despair, and confusion to cloud any decision making during a conflict.

■ Emotions drive people to say what they didn't precisely mean, thereby further escalating a conflict.

■ Emotions incite people to act on the spur of the moment without forethought on the consequences of their actions and anything they say.

Additional barriers continued

3   UNDEFINED JOB DESCRIPTIONS, EXPECTATIONS
Too many offices fail to define what constitutes acceptable
behavior in the workplace. They also don't provide clearly
defined job descriptions that spell out what people are
expected to produce. Workers are much happier when they
know where they stand. Many conflicts can be avoided with
clarity and openness.

- When there are clear job descriptions, no one worker can
  feel aggrieved over his workload, compared with those of
  his fellow workers.

- No single worker or team always gets the new and
  interesting assignments.

4 MISUNDERSTANDING OTHER PEOPLE'S MOTIVATIONS

The distorted view of others' motivations and behavior is arguably one of the biggest stumbling blocks to constructive conflict resolution. This distortion can be caused by

■ **MIRROR IMAGE**
This describes the perception that the other person represents the exact opposite. If you, for instance, feel that you are "in the right," then the other person must necessarily be "in the wrong."

■ **TUNNEL VISION**
This describes how people can form judgments about others without looking at the wider picture and putting other people's behavior into context.

■ **POLARIZED THINKING**
This refers to two people thinking in completely polar ways, obsessed with spotting the differences in values and needs, rather than working on the potential similarities.

Overview of barriers

WHAT ARE COMMON OBSTACLES TO CONFLICT RESOLUTION?

1 DENIAL/AVOIDANCE

A leading barrier to resolving a conflict is to deny that the conflict even exists.

WHY PEOPLE USE DENIAL/AVOIDANCE?
- Fear of upsetting colleagues
- Dislike of change
- Procrastination

2 AGGRESSION

When an aggressive person seeks to win an argument or a point at the expense of someone else, the aggrieved party is likely to respond with anger, resentment, and fear.

WHY PEOPLE USE AGGRESSION?
- Corporate culture. Many large companies favor swift action and resolution over long-term strategy.
- Feelings of inferiority. Aggression can raise self-esteem.
- Compensating for passive behavior. Some passive people who have taken on more work than they can handle may express sudden outbursts of anger.

3 ACCOMMODATION

Accommodating behavior involves putting other people's needs in front of your own.

WHY ACCOMMODATION?
- People think that by pleasing others, their needs will be looked after in the future. People may fear being rejected or of being branded a difficult team player.
- Low self-esteem can lead people to avoid the spotlight at work.

4 COMPROMISE

Compromise involves two or more people making a series of tradeoffs.

WHY COMPROMISE?
- Many people opt for the easy life.
- Coming to a solution, however imperfect, often seems far better than delaying conflict unnecessarily.
- Pragmatic workers can perceive that some objectives have to be adjusted according to circumstances. It's better to be flexible and achieve some gains than to risk losing everything

OVERVIEW

5

resolving conflict

Resolution strategies

The core of this chapter advocates collaboration as the strategy that produces the most satisfying and lasting solution to a conflict. It looks in turn at

- How to improve communication skills that help the collaboration process

- Why collaboration works

- The different stages of the collaboration process

The communication skills that will be considered are

- Listening

- Speaking

Collaboration works when disputing parties

- See conflict as positive

- Can see the dispute from the other person's viewpoint

- Are forward looking

- Make conflict solving a habit

Collaboration is not the only way of resolving conflict and is not necessarily always the most appropriate way so the chapter begins by exploring the two other main strategies for handling conflict

■ Exercising rights: what it is, the pros and cons, and why it might be used

■ Exercising power: what it is, the pros and cons, and why it might be used

The chapter ends with a step-by-step case study of the various layers that may exist in even the most straightforward looking conflict, and looks in turn at the ways that collaboration might solve the problem, given that both parties wish to do so.

Exercise of rights: what is it?

Managers and employees turn to "rights" during a dispute when either party knows that they can win an argument by referring to a company or government policy stipulating their rights that proves that they are officially correct. One example of this is when an employee feels he is unfairly dismissed or passed over for promotion and can prove it. There have been a growing number of cases recently of women and older people who have proven that they have been unfairly passed over for a job as a result of their gender or age. Similarly, there have been high-profile lawsuits in which older employees won their cases against former employers by proving that their contracts were terminated on the grounds of their age.

1 PROS OF APPROACH
The outcome of the dispute is clear-cut. It is sanctioned by a third party.

■ In the case of a company dispute, this could be a senior manager, with or without the input of the human resources department.

■ If it goes to court, the third party would most typically be a judge, sometimes with a jury too.

2 CONS OF APPROACH
In cases where the two parties continue to work together, resentment may linger because there has been a definite winner and a clear loser.

Rights of employees

1 OFFICIAL RIGHTS

By law, private and state companies are obliged to write down basic job rights in job contracts. These include four basic rights:

■ The right to a contract of employment

■ The right to a comprehensive account of working conditions

■ The right to maternity leave, and the company's provisions

■ The right to a statement of the company's redundancy procedures and payments

2

UNOFFICIAL RIGHTS
These cover areas that companies choose to take up as incentives for employees or for ethical reasons. They include:

- The right to study in company time whether by making up for officially lost time or by arranging a change in salary or even without loss of pay

- The right to a sabbatical (paid or unpaid) after a certain period of time in employment

- The right to a job appraisal

Causes of conflict

Some employment contracts leave work duties deliberately vague to give both parties more room for flexibility. Perhaps once an employee's strengths become apparent, the job description can be fleshed out. However, many future disputes could be settled more easily and quickly if job descriptions and duties are clearly spelled out. Those with good negotiation skills may even request special sections to be included in a contract.

FOR MANAGERS
Conflict can occur when managers find that employees are not complying with terms in the employment contract. A list of typical responsibilities can include:

1 To work the full hours you are paid for or to make provisions to compensate for any time taken off at work.

2 To meet deadlines agreed in advance.

3 To give reasonable and justified notice if any goals cannot be adequately met.

4 To take no more than the allocated holiday time.

5 To make requested changes to your work if standards haven't been met.

6 For managers, to provide the appropriate supervision to employees.

7 To admit to mistakes when they have been made and to rectify them.

8 To put the interests of the company before your own.

9 To follow the organization's rules and policies.

10 To work in harmony with colleagues.

Causes of conflict continued

FOR EMPLOYEES

When employees believe managers are demanding too much of their time or forcing them into activities that are not part of their remit, it helps if they can refer to parts of the contract that specify details to questions such as:

1 Is a list of daily duties clearly spelled out? Is there room for misinterpretation in some of the wording so that extra or unrelated work cannot be piled on without the employee's consent?

2 Is the employee specified to work a certain number of hours?

3 Is there a provision to work from home if the situation arises?

4 Does the employee have one or more line managers?

5 How many people are under the employee's supervision?

6 Do I have a right to participate in any decisions that may affect my job?

7 Does the employee have a right to bonuses? How is the bonus worked out?

8 Is there a system of warnings for committing mistakes?

9 What room will the employee have to set his or her own agenda?

10 Does the employee have a right to a pay raise based on performance? How often can he or she expect to get pay raises?

11 Is there a policy for use of internet or the phone for personal use during working hours?

12 Is there a sick-leave policy that differs from rules set by the state?

Exercise of power

WHAT IS IT?

Exercising power is the most traditional and ancient practice in the workplace. It means that the person who enjoys the greatest power and authority (most commonly, senior managers or supervisors) wins the dispute by pulling rank or using aggressive behavior. The explicit belief in this tactic is that "might is right." The abuse of power in companies is one of the reasons why a list of rights was introduced in the workplace to protect the weaker members of the workforce.

PROS OF APPROACH

1 The outcome is clear-cut, as in the process of exercising rights.

2 In spite of new employees' rights, many companies try to bypass technicalities present in contracts, relying on employees' ignorance of their rights and their fear of losing their jobs in a competitive marketplace.

CONS OF APPROACH

1
As there is no legal sanctioning of a dispute that is settled through "power" tactics, the conflict can always flare up again. There can also be a lasting resentment in the office when someone has clearly squashed another worker's challenge.

2
In the case of a conflict between two people who are equally powerful in the company hierarchy, a dispute based on a power struggle can easily end up in a stalemate, with both sides losing.

3
When the focus becomes who wins and who loses, such questions as "what is the best course of action" or "what will make the most difference to our bottom line" are lost.

Exercise of power continued

TYPICAL FEATURES OF WINNERS AND POWER STRUGGLES

1 They are generally people with higher status in the company.

2 Their goals are highly important, and they will do anything to achieve their objectives.

3 They are not interested in others' needs or rights.

4 They are not concerned about whether people like them or not.

5 They may lose focus on what is good for the company in their pursuit of winning.

TYPICAL FEATURES OF LOSERS OF POWER STRUGGLES

1 They are generally people lower down the pecking order of the company.

2 When the people have the same status within the company, they tend to avoid conflict because they place a greater premium on achieving harmony at work.

3 They are pessimistic about the outcomes of a conflict, and they don't even know whether they have any right to challenge the aggressor.

4 They don't put a high premium on their objectives.

5 They show more concern for other people's needs than their own.

Exercise of power continued

It is useful to recognize the various tactics or games used by people who choose to exercise power. Take the following scenario:

CASE STUDY

Three middle managers at a financial services company are debating the launch of a new mortgage product to their clients. The most forceful manager is pressing for a swift launch to catch competitors unaware. The other two are more hesitant, preferring to do some more research.

The following approaches describe some of the most common gambits of the forceful manager:

1. SETTING AN AGENDA

At the meeting, the "power" player quickly establishes his needs and objectives and make these the source of discussion. "You all know what I think of this new product. It provides us with an excellent opportunity. I'm sure we all agree with that." Watch out too for:

1

FORCEFUL INSTRUCTIONS
The person will try and control others through the use of
commands like "It has to be done immediately" or warnings
like "The company stands to lose if we don't act now."

2

OPINIONS DISGUISED AS FACTS
The person's judgment will be expressed as a fact: "Everyone
knows that the mortgage market is changing faster than ever
before" or "Ask anyone and they'll tell you the same."

3

HEAVY USE OF "I" STATEMENT
Although "I" statements used at appropriate moments are
assertive, when they are used liberally they indicate a self-
centered speaker. Phrases like "I know it will work" and "In
my experience, that's always been the case with product
launches" are aimed at discouraging any challenge.

Exercise of power continued

2. REFUTING OTHER AGENDAS
In the event of a challenge, "power" players will counter the views of others and try to trash them using a variety of tactics, such as pouring blame, making rhetorical comments, and offering strong advice.

1 UNFOCUSED CRITICISM
Beware of critical statements that rarely tend to focus on a specific subject. This makes it more difficult to argue against them. "You are responsible for the company losing that account," for example. Power brokers do not focus on possible contributing factors such as "you did not provide the necessary figures in good time" or "your report was two days late," but on bigger issues that are not easy to break down.

2   RHETORICAL COMMENTS
These tend to be based on assumptions that the other person
has done something wrong. For instance "I suppose you've
forgotten to include the latest hike in interests into the
discussion" or "You obviously haven't read the latest
predictions on the housing market."

3   STRONG ADVICE
Aggressive people never miss an opportunity to give advice
that tends to be in the form of "I know better." For instance,
"Your vision of the market is rather outdated. You should read
what's been happening in California. The trend ought to
spread to the rest of the country."

Exercise of power continued

3. FORCING THE OTHER'S HAND

Finally, the "power" player will do his or her best to force through a fast decision. There are three basic ways in which this might be attempted, through imposing a time limit, dismissing alternatives, and offering, usually spurious trade-offs.

1 IMPOSING A TIME LIMIT
Stating or even implying that not acting immediately could have serious consequences is a major gambit of the "power" player. He or she may use such phrases as "I've heard that two of our competitors are looking to launch a similar product. We will be playing catch-up if we wait any longer."

2 DISMISSING ALTERNATIVES

Without giving due consideration to alternatives, whether these have been discussed previously or not, the "power" player will attempt to present his or her solution as the only way forward. Watch out for such phrases as "We've gone through all the facts and there really isn't any alternative."

3 OFFERING TRADE-OFFS

The final play in this type of scenario is to suggest that, in return for swift agreement, the power player is giving way on another point, usually of little relevance. "If we push this through, we can look at that other issue you mentioned."

Collaboration

WHAT IS IT?

Collaborating describes the process of solving a conflict in a way that both parties can believe that they have gained something and can move forward in a positive fashion. In contrast to exercising "power" or "rights," it involves exercising "mutual interests." This book advocates collaboration over other approaches to resolving differences because it represents an "ideal" way of relating to others. However, it recognizes that in the messy workplace, there are few occasions when, however much both parties are committed to try (and that in itself is a big task in some organizations), there isn't an element of "power" or "rights" tactics at play.

The following points summarize the principal features of the collaborative process, several of which are described in more detail in the remaining pages of this chapter.

1. TAKING A POSITIVE ATTITUDE

A belief in collaboration implies a positive attitude toward disagreement because there is a fundamental trust in being able to resolve differences. The focus is not only in the fact of reaching a settlement, which after all can be achieved in some cases by coercion or by settling in court, but on leaving both parties as satisfied by both the process and the outcome.

The underlying assumption is that conflict can force people to be creative and challenge others into new ways of thinking and novel ways of acting. Conflict can thus be a positive force for change. Through working together to solve a disagreement, a team may become stronger and more cohesive, rather than less.

Collaboration continued

2. WEARING SOMEONE ELSE'S LENSES

Trying to come to a mutual agreement implies trying to see things from someone else's perspective. The mere act of being able to adopt a different point of view predisposes a person to seeing that there are many more ways of resolving an issue than they imagined. It may even prevent you as manager from forcing through a solution that you thought was beneficial to you but in fact, on reflection, doesn't make business sense in the long run.

Considering the reasons for an opponent's position

- Fosters team building

- Forces you to consider possible alternatives

- Demonstrates a commitment to finding a solution

3. LOOKING FORWARD

Many conflicts occur in the workplace where the main participants in a dispute don't have the privilege of walking away after an outcome has been established. Even when someone wins a battle against a colleague, it doesn't mean the solution is sure to be long-lasting. The winner may still lose the war.

When negotiating an outcome, it is useful to think what the long term consequences are for you in the office, how both people will work together on another project, how others will view you if you end up as the outright winner or loser.

4. ADOPTING CONFLICT SOLVING AS A HABIT

Even when you win a conflict through an exercise of power, the antagonistic process for most people is generally off-putting. However, resolving conflicts through collaboration can be remembered as a positive team-building experience. Once achieved successfully, it can become easier to implement again, thereby reducing the aggravation and time wasting that future conflicts (and they will appear!) bring.

Sharpening collaborative skills

Before embarking on the process of collaboration, it is important to review the skills necessary to negotiate effectively. It is arguable that the most important skill is communication.

THE ART OF LISTENING
First, it is useful to be aware of ways of listening that are not conducive to effective communication in the workplace (and elsewhere).

1 FOCUSING ON OTHER'S RIGHTS
Some people are so worried about what others think about them or how they are expected to respond that they focus on their own behavior rather than on really listening to what others are saying.

2 FOCUSING TOO MUCH ON OWN RIGHTS

There are two problems with the listening skills of people who tend to think too much about their own rights and their side of the argument:

■ They are generally concerned with what they are going to say next and do not actively listen to what the other person is saying.

■ Just as they tend to have fixed opinions, they are also selective listeners, picking on words that will support their interpretation of what is being said rather than actually listening to the words.

The signs that they are not listening properly are

■ A lack of eye contact

■ Few visual signs of listening such as gentle nodding of the head

■ Frequent interruptions

Tips for effective listening

1 MAKE EYE CONTACT
Have you ever tried to tell someone something important, and their eyes are wandering around the room or they are busy skim reading a report? To avoid this off-putting habit, make sure you maintain regular eye contact with the speaker but don't fix your gaze constantly as this becomes intimidating.

2 ENCOURAGE
Make intermittent gestures to show you are following the speaker. Gestures include smiling, saying "yes" and "no," raising eyebrows to show surprise, and nodding. Avoid the tendency to exaggerate the gestures as they will suggest you are actually bored.

3   TAKE NOTES (MENTALLY)
Try to draw out a few main points from the speaker's exchange as this will help you sort out what is important about the speaker's message. Distinguish between facts and opinions. If the speaker is rambling or nervous and the messages are unclear, you can ask yourself a few questions to get a clearer picture: "Why is he telling me this now?" and "How is he feeling about telling me this?"

4   PARAPHRASE
When the speaker has finished, you can show you have been actively listening by repeating back in your own words, and rather more briefly, the main points. This is also a way of checking that you have understood the other person.

Tips for effective listening continued

5 KNOW WHEN TO INTERRUPT
In principle, it is better to keep interruptions to a minimum as they stop the natural flow of the speaker. Frequent interruptions also tend to give the impression that you don't want to listen and are too focused on your own needs.
  Sometimes, though, it is necessary to interject. These are the occasions when it is acceptable:

■ If the speaker is veering off the subject, you may intervene with a few key words of the main message to get the speaker back on track.

■ If you violently disagree with a statement or opinion that is not part of the main message you may want to make your viewpoint clear.

■ If you want to verify that you have understood a specific part of the argument that needs clearing up immediately.

6 LIMIT OPINIONS
Unless you have been asked specifically for an opinion, don't
feel compelled to come up with a solution or immediate
response. Imparting advice can come across as bossy or
intrusive or both.

7 AVOID HOOKS
Even though listening and responding sympathetically to
other viewpoints are parts of assertive listening, there are
some potential dangers. The speaker may try to weaken your
own point of view and try to pull you into their logic. They may
also try to sidetrack you from the main business you are trying
to focus on. These gambits are also called hooks. The most
effective way of not getting hooked is to paraphrase back
what the person is telling you to show that you are listening
and then to use a core phrase that outlines your position. That
tells the speaker you are not prepared to be drawn into an
argument or to labor over an irrelevant point at this stage.

Tips for effective listening continued

8

SHOW EMPATHY
Empathy is your ability to recognize the feelings of others,
and feel them for yourself. If you feel empathy with
someone, you understand their wants and needs, and their
way of thinking. Try to cast your own views aside for a while
and concentrate on seeing the situation from the other
person's point of view (this is often referred to as "putting
yourself in someone else's shoes"). Showing empathy is
sometimes referred to as "nondirective listening" because
you are literally not directing or channeling the other person's
thought in any direction. You are giving the person the respect
to find his or her own direction. The other person may have
no specific objective other than to unload how he or she is
currently feeling.

9 MATCH OR MIRROR

Empathetic listening can sometimes lead to making subtle adjustments to your own behavior to blend in as much as possible with the other speaker. This does not mean relinquishing your own views or personality. If done skillfully, it can be a way of creating a closer rapport with the speaker. Matching or blending involves:

■ Quickly identifying the language of the other person

■ Identifying the speed of the delivery

■ Noting the loudness of the voice

For instance, if you are dealing with a soft-spoken person who likes to think before speaking and has a slow delivery, you may have to tone down your naturally loud, fast way of talking. People are far more likely to respect your views when you mirror and match them.

Tips for effective speaking

DOING THE TALKING

In addition to listening effectively, communicating your point of view in a clear, concise, and nonthreatening manner is just as important a skill in the collaborative process. These are some tips to follow to express yourself effectively.

1

PREPARE BRIEF, CORE PHRASE

Speaking in clear, direct, unambiguous sentences helps the assertive person put across his or her point effectively. Think of a core phrase that expresses your message in as few words as possible. Get rid of any padding. If you have various messages, form several core phrases.

2 DON'T ASSUME
Never assume that other people automatically have the same points of reference as you. You can't expect other people to read your mind. It's better to spell things out in detail than to withhold information.

3 USE "I" STATEMENTS
Using "I" statements can be confused with aggression and a strong ego, but this applies only when they are accompanied with unreasonable or dismissive opinions and relayed in a loud tone of voice. Otherwise, an "I" statement shows that the speaker takes full responsibility for his opinion. For instance, "I think it is a good idea" defines the speaker's opinion more clearly and decisively than "Don't you think it's a good idea?" Other instances of "I" statements such as "I feel angry when..." or "I want..." show conviction and directness. There is no intention of hiding behind bland statements such as "The company believes it is better...."

Tips for effective speaking continued

4 AVOID JARGON
People who keep changing their words and phrases according to the people they are talking to are sometimes accused of being inconsistent. However if you want to make your message clear, you should be aware of the speaker and change your vocabulary if the other person may be unfamiliar with certain technical or management jargon. Creating a gap between the speaker and the receiver or listener is hardly effective communication.

5 ASK QUESTIONS
To show that you respect the rights of others, effective communicators don't just make direct, honest statements. They ask questions to find out what others think. They ask leading questions that will encourage others to express their opinions.

6

AVOID GENERALIZATIONS
Don't assume that everyone thinks alike, and avoid sweeping
statements like "most people would agree that" or "everyone
knows that this won't work." Show that you are able to
distinguish between opinions and facts, and encourage others
to do the same.

7

MAKE SUGGESTIONS
You may already have made up your mind on an issue, but
avoid heavy-handed advice like "It's clearly better to...." Try
instead: "Do you think it would be better if...." That allows the
other people to make up their own minds

Collaboration in action

This next section describes the four main stages during a collaborative process. These steps are mainly guidelines, they are not prescriptive, and the order in which they occur will vary significantly from one conflict situation to another.

1. THE APPROACH

1

ADMIT THAT THERE IS A CONFLICT

There are many reasons for denying or ignoring a conflict at work (see Chapter 4, pp. 102–105), so arriving at the moment of admitting there is a problem is not as easy as it sounds. However, for any resolution process to begin, this is the necessary starting point. Ideally, both participants will come to that conclusion at the same time but that almost never happens so as the ideal "conflict manager," you should be the one who brings the delicate subject up.

2 ADDRESS THE PERSON

Having admitted to yourself that the conflict is serious, you should approach the person with whom you have the disagreement. It is best to do this in private and in person. Sending an email, however tempting, can appear distant. By seeing the person, you can gauge his or her response much quicker. Make sure you are ready to go to the person in a spirit of humility and understanding. If you find yourself about to give a lecture or force the person to the negotiating table, you should abandon the idea.

3 BE READY FOR THE WORST

It would be ideal if the other person agreed with you that it is "high time we talk and yes I'm so glad you came to see me." In the real world, you may be rebutted with an "I really don't see any point in talking about this" or even worse, be received with blank indifference: "I really don't know what you are fussing about. Everything is fine." You may have to ask a colleague or senior manager to approach the person on a separate occasion to reason with him or her. The most likely outcome is that you may have to wait until the other person is ready to talk.

Collaboration in action continued

4 BE READY FOR THE BEST
You may be taken by surprise and come to a mutual
agreement about the need for a meeting. Be ready for that
eventuality and have a few proposals up your sleeve.

■ Suggest (never order or demand) a couple of alternative
venues for a meeting. Choose venues that are both neutral
and private.

■ Suggest a couple of times that you think might be suitable
for both of you.

■ End your suggestion by asking whether the other party
has any alternative ideas. You want to show at this stage
that you are open to suggestions.

5 ESTABLISH GROUND RULES

You could wait until the actual meeting, but it is probably best to suggest ground rules at this stage to give both parties time to evaluate and perhaps add to them. Simple ground rules might include:

■ One person will speak at a time.

■ Each person will listen to the other with respect.

■ Any conversation will be kept confidential.

■ We will refer to any existing "resolution" guidelines at the office.

Collaboration in action continued

2. THE MEETING: IDENTIFYING NEEDS

This section focuses on the importance of identifying the real issues causing the conflict.

Assume that the present disagreement is between two colleagues, of equal ranking, who are fighting over taking extra time off around the Thanksgiving holiday. The department cannot be left without one or the other as supervisor for longer than the holiday weekend itself. It transpires that the more aggressive person has booked a two-week vacation around Thanksgiving without mentioning it to his colleague who then explains that she was also planning to take time off during that exact period. She has a large family and can only take a vacation then, when the rest of her family can get together. He is single and could take a vacation any other time.

Ostensibly, this a fairly clear-cut conflict: she is angry because his booking of the vacation without mentioning his plans now makes it virtually impossible for her to request taking that time off too. In fact, however, there are deeper frustrations at play.

Her male colleague frequently makes decisions in the department without asking for her opinion even though they are both senior managers and share equal responsibility for the running of the department. He does this repeatedly, not only in booking vacations (and this has happened before) but with more strategic business decisions. She feels undermined and threatened by this behavior, which she believes could lead to a diminishing role in the department for her.

Collaboration in action continued

1 PUT COMMUNICATION SKILLS INTO PRACTICE
If the woman is determined not to give in on this occasion, she
needs to remain calm and assertive, spelling out her needs clearly
by using "I" statements. This is a chance for the man to describe his
colleague's position or feelings. He could begin with "As I see it, you
feel I always take time off at inconvenient times...." Even though she
feels she is in the right, she should make the effort to listen to his
explanation for having booked a vacation without consulting her.
She might be surprised with his explanation. He could respond that
"You never make any decisions until the last minute and get irritated
if you are pressed too many times. I've tried to talk to you about
vacation bookings before, and you never know your plans. That's
why I'm forced to take decisions on my own." If this is true, she
may have identified that he has his own issues with her working
practices, beyond the vacation issue. Her feedback could run along
the lines of: "So what I understand is that you don't think I make
my intentions clear enough and leave things to the last minute?"
The seeds for bringing up some fundamentals about their
working relationship and doing something to break the stalemate
appear to be there.

2   **FOCUS ON ISSUES, NOT PERSONALITIES**

It is important at this stage, for both sides to stick rigidly to the issues and not to turn this dispute into a personal slinging match. For instance, it would be negative for the man to accuse the woman of "always leaving things to the last minute" because that is a direct criticism of her whole person and is likely to be met by a hostile response, full of self-justification. He would be better off saying that "the fact that you couldn't decide about your vacation plans last month made it difficult for me to make any arrangements." This tells her two things:

■ It identifies the impact of her behavior on him.

■ It focuses on the vacation issue, rather than opening up a debate about her general indecision. That matter could be tackled at a later, less sensitive date.

Collaboration in action continued

3. GENERATING OPTIONS

1. REVIEW ISSUES, NEEDS

Before considering the options available to them, the work colleagues who are disputing their vacation schedules should check that they understand the issues at stake. These are the questions that they should ask themselves:

1 Having listened to you, what do I understand as our real areas of difference, compared with our perceived differences before we spoke?

2 Am I defining the problem in similar terms? Are our needs similar (that is, the actual Thanksgiving break), or do we have different priorities about the problems that need to be solved?

3 Do I need any additional information before I can start to examine possible solutions?

4 THE MAN
At this stage, the man may choose to focus on this specific vacation case and not bring other decision-making issues into the argument, fearing that it will present a major stumbling block to a resolution.

5 THE WOMAN
She may decide that it is too sensitive to mention his authoritarian tendencies in other aspects of their work and that she is better off fighting this specific battle. If she makes inroads with this issue, maybe she will gain confidence to tackle other aspects of their working relationship in a more opportune moment.

Collaboration in action continued

2. BRAINSTORM

Agree to spend at least ten minutes exploring several options. You might agree to voice them in turn or to spend some time scribbling them out and then reading them aloud.

You could always read each other's options aloud. It is surprising how different your own suggestions sound when they come out of the supposed "enemy's" mouth.

The different options suggested could include:

1
THE MAN

■ To keep his vacation given that he has already paid for it and promise the woman first choice for dates around the next major holiday weekend.

■ To change the return date of his vacation (this may incur fewer charges) and split the vacation between the two.

■ To force her to stick to the decision and teach her to think more about forward planning.

2 THE WOMAN
- For him to cancel his vacation and let his cancellation charges remind him of the importance of consulting others in the future.

- To let him go on his vacation and demand some sort of bonus (an extra day's leave) for her good faith.

- To request that a senior supervisor act as an arbitrator of the matter. The company may have experienced a similar disagreement in the past.

Collaboration in action continued

4. AGREEING TO SOLUTIONS

1. KEEP OPINIONS PRIVATE

When the options have been aired, it is important for neither party to say which option they prefer at this stage or to express outrage at any of the proposals. This is a time for quiet consideration from both parties. Even if the parties have already come to a conclusion, they should show each other that they are taking the other options into account. It is best practice to go through each option and assign it a score between one and ten. This ensures that every option is carefully considered before comparisons between them are made.

2. EXAMINE ALTERNATIVE SCENARIOS

Before assigning final scores, the parties may be helped in their decision by looking at the alternative scenarios to not reaching an agreement. The alternatives to negotiating are commonly divided into three broad categories:

1

BEST ALTERNATIVE TO A NEGOTIATED AGREEMENT (BATNA)
What is the best each person can expect if they don't come
to a negotiated agreement?

THE MAN
He wants this vacation but will agree to give her first choice
next time.

THE WOMAN
She will forgo this vacation but wants assurance from him
about future decisions, both about vacations and other
departmental matters.

Collaboration in action continued

2 WORST ALTERNATIVE TO A NEGOTIATED AGREEMENT (WATNA)
What is the worst each can expect if they don't come to a
negotiated agreement?

THE MAN
She may insist on taking that time off and the matter will
have to be resolved by human resources or a senior manager.
This could be rather humiliating.

THE WOMAN
He insists on taking his vacation break, and she is forced to
give in again.

3 MOST LIKELY ALTERNATIVE TO A NEGOTIATED AGREEMENT (MLATNA)
What is the most likely alternative if they don't come to a
negotiated agreement?

Historically, she has given in to his demands and way of
working but she is not prepared to settle for the most likely
scenario based on previous behavior patterns.

EVALUATE OPTIONS
Both parties should revise each other's preferred options, and
look at the respective scores assigned to each proposal. By
now, if there is room for agreement, it should be clear what
items they agree on. For instance, neither wants this to go to
arbitration by human resources because it would reflect badly
on both. Accepting the status quo (that is, that he goes on the
vacation without making concessions) also scores low. It
emerges that a compromise where he goes on vacation and
she receives promises of future choices is the most popular.
She is happy because she has aired an important grievance,
until now kept under wraps. Her frustration is gone. She is
ready to be more assertive and has taken on board the need to
improve her forward planning. She also feels more confident
about tackling other work disagreements with him in the
future without seeing it as a win or lose situation.

Collaboration in action continued

WHAT HAPPENS WHEN THERE IS NO AGREEMENT?

In real life, the ideal scenario is often difficult to achieve. It is quite possible that the resentment built up by the woman in the Thanksgiving vacation case is so extreme that she can't compromise at all (this incident is the final straw in their continued conflict). Or the man may show no willingness to give up his vacation plans or to acknowledge that his plans and other behaviors are upsetting her. These are the two potential scenarios ensuing from this present impasse.

1. ARBITRATION/MEDIATION

It may have reached the stage that there are now only two possible scenarios:

■ He agrees to cancel his vacation, regardless of the costs involved.

■ She takes the matter to the human resources department or their senior director to decide on.

As the aggrieved party, it is up to her to decide on this course of action. She should take into account that even if he is forced to give up his vacation as a result of the mediation or arbitration process (discussed in Chapter 6), the seeds of the conflict will continue. In fact, their working relationship will have deteriorated still further because he is likely to feel humiliated by the decision.

Collaboration in action continued

2. SOLDIERING ON

Most workplace issues do have solutions, however intractable the disputes may seem to the parties during the height of a conflict. The other alternative to mediation, apart from ignoring the problem (and by now, this is too late), is to return to the resolution process. These are some recommended steps.

1 ARRANGE ANOTHER MEETING
Both sides may need time to review their options and consider more carefully what the implications of a stalemate might be.

2 REFRAME THE ISSUE
Both parties may look at the Thanksgiving vacation conflict and consider what deeper issues are at stake. Until now, they have both chosen not to bring the issues of "late decision making" and "no consultation" into the frame. But maybe a broader discussion about their working relationship will now be possible and valuable.

3 SEEK INFORMAL MEDIATION
Both parties might try going through the meeting and the issues with an objective third party who is not assuming the role of mediator but merely providing off-the-record advice.

4 SEEK AREAS OF AGREEMENT
Maybe in the heat of the moment, the parties overlooked points that both agreed on. It is useful to go through the list of options and explore these points again.

5 EXPLORE ALTERNATIVES
Going through the best, worst, and most likely scenarios if negotiation doesn't take place can act as a sobering reality check for both sides. Facing these alternatives may encourage both sides to be more flexible.

Overview of conflict resolution

WHY CAN COLLABORATION PROVE THE BEST STRATEGY?

■ Both parties can feel that they have gained something.
■ There is a fundamental trust in being able to resolve differences.
■ Trying to come to a mutual agreement forces parties to see the problem from the other person's perspective and fosters creativity and team spirit.

WHAT ARE THE MAIN STAGES OF COLLABORATION?

1 THE APPROACH
■ You have to admit the conflict.
■ You have to approach the person with whom you have the disagreement.
■ You have to establish ground rules for a meeting.

2 THE MEETING: IDENTIFYING NEEDS
■ Put your communication skills to practice. Use clear "I" statements to explain your stance. Provide feedback on what the other person is telling you.
■ Try to stick rigidly to the issues and not turn this dispute into a personal slinging match.

3 GENERATING OPTIONS

■ Review the issues and needs. Ask yourself questions like: What are the real areas or difference as opposed to perceived areas of differences? Are we defining the problem in similar terms?

■ Brainstorm for more options. You could always read each other's options to the other. It is surprising how different one's own suggestions sound when they are voiced by the supposed enemy.

4 AGREEING TO SOLUTIONS

1. Keep opinions private. Go through each option and assign it a score between one and ten. This ensures that every option is considered.

2. Examine alternative scenarios:

■ What is the best each person can expect if they don't come to a negotiated agreement?

■ What is the worst each can expect if they don't come to a negotiated agreement?

■ What is the most likely alternative if they don't come to a negotiated agreement?

■ Evaluate options. Both parties should revise each other's preferred options, and look at the respective scores assigned to each proposal.

OVERVIEW

6

making mediation work

Introduction to mediation

This chapter examines

- What mediation is and what its main benefits are, beginning with a comparison with another widely used conflict resolution process, arbitration

- When it might be necessary to seek mediation to resolve a conflict or dispute

- What the role of a mediator is, and the type of people who might be best qualified to fulfill this role

- What the four main stages in the mediation process are

WHAT MEDIATION IS NOT

ARBITRATION

It is useful to begin defining mediation by examining another process that is often confused with mediation: arbitration.

The terms are used misleadingly, for two main reasons:

- The main reason is that both processes involve a third party who is called in to settle a dispute between two conflicting sides who cannot reach a satisfactory agreement between themselves.

- In addition, both occur outside the courtroom.

However, the similarities end here. These are some of the most common features of arbitration.

1 LEGALLY BINDING

Unlike mediation, which occurs in a more informal setting, arbitration is a judicial process in which both sides leave the final decision to a third party. They enter the process knowing they have to abide by the final decision.

What mediation is not

2 WIN-LOSE SCENARIO
Unlike mediation, where the process aims at trying to reach an agreement that will partly benefit both sides, arbitration is more adversarial. Both sides have to be prepared to end up as a winner and a loser, depending on the decision.

3 MORE COSTLY
Because of the legally binding nature of arbitration, it is common that arbitration leads to significantly more substantial costs, particularly if a decision leads to one party taking legal action or litigation. Typically, even when arbitration is supposed to avoid litigation, the process can end up involving lawyers, motions, briefs, judges, and awards for damages, all of which are costly.

4

COMMERCIAL, NOT PERSONAL
Disputes that require arbitration are far more likely to involve commercial partners than family businesses, although there are exceptions. The main reason for this is that arbitration deals directly with the facts of the case, not taking into account any of the emotional aspects of a dispute, which are far more common in a family business.

5

PROTRACTED
Conflicts that end up going to arbitration are normally long-winded and protracted because other avenues of reaching agreement, such as mediation, have failed.

Benefits of arbitration

These are the principle advantages of using arbitration:

1 REMOVES PERSONAL EMOTIONS
Personal emotions in a conflict can never disappear, but the arbitration process does help to keep emotions on the back burner because the emphasis is on the facts. The fact that both parties have agreed to go to arbitration is a tacit admission that they have failed to agree, which is, in itself, a positive development from merely disagreeing and being unable to find a way forward.

2 BINDS IN LAW
Even if disagreement continues after the final decision, both parties have to agree by law on the outcome.

3 ESTABLISHES EQUAL PARITY
Many disputes continue because one side feels the other is using more power and money to put across his or her position. The arbitration process insists on giving each side equal opportunities to defend their arguments, so both parties know they are treated even-handedly.

4 PROVIDES A FIXED TIMETABLE
The schedule of an arbitration process is commonly fixed so that a decision has to be made within a reasonable period of time. This contrasts with the mediation process, which continues for as long as both parties feel necessary to come to some agreement.

Drawbacks of arbitration

The following are disadvantages of using arbitration.

1 HEIGHTENS ENEMY POSITIONS
The fixed timetable of the process encourages both sides to step up their positions to make their cases as clearly and powerfully as possible. The win-lose scenario also helps to create the adversarial atmosphere of the proceedings.

2 ASSIGNS HIGH COSTS TO LOSER
The inevitable win-lose scenario means that the party that loses the case is liable for hefty payments to pay for damages or compensation, not to mention the legal fees of the process.

3 CREATES PERSONAL DISSATISFACTION
Because the process deliberately steers away from any
emotional issues in a dispute, these personal elements are not
catered for during or after the process. It can leave both sides,
particularly the losing party, with no ways of dealing with any
emotional fallout of the final decision.

4 DOES NOT ALLOW FOR FLEXIBILITY
The time boundaries of the process and the legally binding
nature of the outcome means there is no turning back at the
end, even when a party strongly believes that there has been
no justice in the decision.

making mediation work

What is mediation?

These are generally held to be the most common features of the process of mediation.

1 ASSISTED NEGOTIATION
The main difference between negotiation and mediation is that the latter involves a third party acting as an observer to existing negotiations.

2 VOLUNTARY
When two conflicting parties agree to turn to mediation, they do so willingly. They are not bound by the process, unlike the case of arbitration. They can stop at any time and resume the process at a later date.

3 PRIVATE, CONFIDENTIAL
Deliberately aimed at keeping a dispute from the public spotlight which can prove costly both to a company's financial accounts and reputation, mediation involves holding talks in private.

4

FOCUSED ON PRESENT
One of the biggest setbacks in any negotiations is the insistence on dwelling on past faults and problems. Mediation tries to focus on the way in which any problem can be resolved today.

5

OBJECTIVE
The best mediation takes place when the third party keeps any personal opinions strictly off the agenda. However tempting it may be, mediation steers away from giving advice to either party. A mediator's most valuable asset is his neutrality.

6

COLLABORATIVE
One of mediation's prime goals is to foster collaboration between parties. A refusal to accept responsibility and to shift blame are two main reasons why parties cannot resolve disputes and why a third party has to be invited to observe their meetings.

What is mediation? continued

7 STAKEHOLDER CONTROLLED
Unlike arbitration, where the final outcome of talks is left to the third party, mediation firmly keeps the decision process in the hands of the stakeholders. Mediators may help sides reevaluate positions and to appreciate the most viable options, but they cannot provide solutions.

8 INFORMAL
Mediation is often conducted in a neutral, non-threatening environment, away from the emotive court room that is a feature of arbitration or litigation.

9 COMMUNICATIVE
A mediator tries to help both sides understand each other's
position and to do so, it has to help the parties put their
arguments across succinctly. The most effective mediation
promotes communication.

10 INEXPENSIVE
Mediation is almost always less costly than going to court. By
attempting to resolve a long-simmering conflict, it may also
end up saving the parties money by freeing up time to focus
on the business .

11 AGREEMENT-ORIENTED
The ultimate objective of mediation is an agreement,
preferably in writing to avoid any future misinterpretations
on what was agreed.

Benefits of mediation

The following are the main advantages of mediation over other methods of conflict resolution:

1 INVITES DEMOCRATIC INVOLVEMENT

In many disputes, there are usually two main adversaries that prevent any possibility of agreement or compromise. This is unfair and frustrating for other participants in the conflict. Through mediation, these people, who are often sidelined as passive bystanders, are encouraged to play a much greater role in the problem-solving process. A mediator tries to hear opinions from all those involved in the fallout from the central characters. This democratization

■ Helps with team building and bonding

■ Ensures that everyone with any involvement in the conflict is heard

2 ENCOURAGES DECISION MAKING

Rather than delivering a verdict from on high, mediation goads the principal participants to come to a decision that best suits all parties. If participants believe they have fought for a decision and feel intimately involved in the process, they are far more likely to respect the outcome and stick to it. A decision that is handed down is less likely to invite participants to buy in, with the result that the conflict cannot be said to be resolved and can easily resurface the next time there is any tension between the protagonists. This scenario also ignores the views of the bystanders to the dispute, who may feel marginalized.

Benefits of mediation continued

3 ALLOWS TIME FOR RESOLUTION
Arbitration imposes a timeframe on resolving a dispute, but mediation is in for the long haul. The process acknowledges that most problems can't be resolved in an hour or two. Often, lengthy sessions across several weeks are necessary for two main reasons:

- To fit in with participants' busy schedules

- To allow sides to come to trust each other

The upside is that once a measure of trust has been established between participants and mediator, progress may be possible.

4   CUTS TO THE CHASE

It is not a contradiction to state that while mediation can allow for a generous timetable to resolve an issue if necessary, it can also ensure a speedy resolution. This is particularly the case when mediators have experience in uncovering hidden agendas and in controlling game playing. Disputes that have been blocked for a long time can be quickly broken down into easy-to-manage sections. Within days, a problem that has festered for years can sometimes be resolved. If smaller issues can be dealt with and solutions found, the larger issues assume less importance and can be dealt with.

Benefits of mediation continued

5 LIMITS COSTS TO COMPANY

The major savings that successful mediation can bring for disputing partners in one business or for two battling companies cannot be overstated. There are two significant ways mediation saves money.

- So many companies become involved in long court cases that end up providing considerable business for lawyers and draining money away from participants' core business.

- Protracted public wrangling results in adverse publicity, which also damages the bottom line. Mediation can resolve conflicts without turning to the legal system.

6 ENCOURAGES CONSTRUCTIVE DIALOG

So many disputes stall because of poor communication or no communication at all. Mediation can break this cycle by

■ Encouraging people to state their cases again

■ Even more importantly, to listen to each other

The best conversations focus on ways in which people can solve problems and move on, rather than dwell on the historical problems themselves.

When is mediation suitable?

Mediation is not necessarily the appropriate way to resolve every conflict. The suitability of mediation will depend on the nature of the disagreement and on the short- and long-term goals of the participants.

This following questionnaire can help you decide whether mediation is suitable to the dispute and to the participants. Try to answer "yes" or "no" to the questions and only look at the scoring system at the end.

SELF-ASSESSMENT QUESTIONNAIRE

1

- Are you ready to invest a reasonable amount of time and energy in resolving this conflict?

- Can you commit several sessions to the issue?

2 Are you happy about airing your grievances about an issue in front of a third party whom you don't necessarily know?

3 Do you want to avoid a legal battle?

4 Is the other party amenable to sitting around a table with a third party?

5
- Are you at all flexible about the final outcome?

- Can you see yourself giving in on any point if it means the other side also retreats in some of their demands?

When is mediation suitable? continued

6 Have you exhausted all other methods of resolving the conflict other than going to court?

7 Is it important that any agreement is made in an atmosphere of privacy?

8 Is it important for you to continue a personal relationship with the person you are disagreeing with after the mediation process is concluded?

9 Are you finding it difficult to put your point across? Can you say honestly that you have been attentive to all the other person's demands?

10 Is the conflict having a negative impact on your business?

SCORE: If you have answered "yes" to at least half the questions, then you and the situation may profit from mediation. If you have answered "no" to more than half, then it appears that you and the other party are not ready for a third-party observer or are not convinced about the benefits of mediation. It could also mean that you have already tried mediation and only arbitration can resolve the conflict.

Who mediates?

Successful mediation will in many ways be the result of choosing the appropriate mediator or group of mediators, depending on the length of time to be spent on the process.

Remember, though, that the suitable mediator for one dispute may not necessarily fit the bill for another kind of conflict. The list of candidates is likely to include the following figures.

1

BUSINESS COLLEAGUE/ASSOCIATE
This could be someone in the company who knows both parties but who is not directly involved in the dispute and doesn't stand to gain personally from the mediation process.

2

MANAGER
In the case of two middle managers, the participation of a senior manager, chosen by both parties, may be appropriate.

3 CONSULTANT
An outside consultant most typically is an expert in your business sector or in other cases like yours. He will usually demand a fee. In a family-run business, where participants are prepared to open up more personally, members could refer to a psychologist.

4 LAWYER/ACCOUNTANT
A professional like a lawyer or accountant, potentially with existing ties with the company, may also be asked to oversee a dispute. Using a company lawyer to mediate at this stage may mean that the more expensive option of arbitration does not become necessary.

How to choose mediators

Not all mediators have experience in former mediation. However, they may share several of the following characteristics.

1

EXPERT IN FIELD

■ When a dispute is particularly technical and the disagreement is over details that are specific to your business sector, then finding a person who has knowledge and experience in your field may prove the best bet.

■ There are also experts in general management issues w can help you even though they are in a completely diffe line of business.

2

IMPARTIAL OBSERVER

Choosing a mediator with objectivity, this doesn't mean simply that they don't stand to gain anything personally the outcome of the mediation. The candidate should be the kind of person who is able to keep his personal opinions to himself when: asking for contributions, listening to points of view, and making decisions. An opinionated person who likes taking a central role in meetings, for example, is unlikely to remain impartial for long.

3 GOOD LISTENER

Choosing a mediator's role is to try to elicit as much information from both sides as possible so he will have to be a good listener. This means he must be able to focus on other people and what they are saying, even if they may find the subject boring. It also entails asking good questions, being alert to pauses, and being sensitive to obstacles. The three factors may prevent one of the parties from disclosing the full information on the dispute.

4 STRATEGIC THINKER

A person who looks at the big picture and is keen on selling goals will be able to see past the current obstacles to focus instead on the ways of finding solutions in the medium and long term. The manager with a vision of how he wants a department to work further down the line is going to make a more effective mediator than someone who does not have this long-term view. In the Thanksgiving vacation outlined in Chapter 5, for example, a mediator may know that in a year's time, there will be four managers instead of only two, so disputes of a "him or me" nature will be less likely.

making mediation work

Mediators: pitfalls to avoid

Assume that you have been chosen to mediate a dispute. Even before beginning the process, be aware of the following pitfalls:

1   PLAYING THE JUDGE
Your role as mediator is to listen to both sides and to help them reach the agreement. You can't suggest a way forward, provide the agreement, or step in to save the day. The participants have to come up with their own conclusion. If they fail to reach an agreement, regardless of the number of hours and amount of energy you have spent in the process, you have to force yourself to walk away from the problem.

2 HAVING AN OPINION
Even if you manage to keep any final judgments to yourself, it is human to have opinions on the mediating process such as

■ Who is presenting the argument better

■ Who is refusing to listen

Try to remain as neutral as possible. Pretend you are listening to each argument for the first time so you aren't influenced by previous Information on the case.

Mediators: pitfalls to avoid continued

3 BECOMING PERSUADED
Remember that the two parties are not trying to convince you but convince each other. Here are the major don'ts:

■ Don't get involved in the argument.

■ Don't respond to the rhetoric used by each party in turn.

This is particularly easy when you hear the first argument. When you come fresh into a conflict, the first impressions will be all the more persuasive. It is not your job to be convinced by arguments, you need only be convinced that they want to find a solution.

4 FOCUSING ON THE PRESENT

One of the main blocks of disputes is when the participants are unable to see past the present conundrum: they rake over what has happened in the past, then stand back to gauge how it is affecting the future. You may be invited by both sides to wade in the storm they are both navigating, but put their present squabbles into context.

■ What are the prospects of the company and the two protagonists if they don't resolve this conflict?

■ Remind yourself of what they could achieve and then remind them about the potentials for resolution.

Mediators: pitfalls to avoid continued

5 FORGETTING HUMAN ELEMENTS

As a bystander, you may find it easy to analyze exactly what needs to be modified in the relationship in front of you to aid the business. But don't ignore the human elements of a dispute; pride and ego have as major a role as whether the dispute makes business sense or not. If you don't take these human elements into account when trying to negotiate, you are likely to fail in helping them reach an agreement. Taking this into account doesn't mean however that you pander to their egos or concerns.

6 FAILING TO ENGAGE THEM

Not only are you trying not to be swayed by any of the arguments presented to you, but your role as mediator requires you to engage and persuade others that negotiating the best possible outcome is in their best interests. You are not there to sell yourself, but you are there to sell the process of mediation for there is a lot of self-satisfaction in witnessing two conflicting parties agreeing on the best way to resolve a dispute, however minimal.

Mediation in action

The following section covers the three main stages of mediation, which are

■ Preparing for the mediation

■ Conducting the mediating

■ Ending mediation.

These approaches are a guideline, the phases are not fixed and can vary in length and order of play according to the particular conflict.

PREPARING THE MEDIATION

THE PROTAGONISTS: WHAT THEY MUST DO

Unless the protagonists are in agreement on the decision to turn to mediation, there is no use going ahead with the process. Even if one of the two parties is sold on the approach, it won't work. Both sides must be convinced about the usefulness of mediation. Only then can they choose the mediator. Again, both parties must trust and have faith in the chosen mediator for the process to have any chance of a successful outcome.

THE MEDIATOR: WHAT HE OR SHE MUST DO

1 EVALUATE CONFLICT
Although the information the mediator has at the outset will
be fairly general, as a mediator you must have some sense of
the conflict and its protagonists to evaluate quickly whether
you think it is worth your time and energy to go ahead.

2 ARRANGE A PRELIMINARY MEETING
The best way to decide about whether to accept the role of
mediator is to arrange preliminary meetings with both sides
separately. Keep these sessions brief because you are seeking
to remain as neutral as possible and don't want to get drawn
to the small details of the case. These sessions are meant to
help the protagonists to gain trust in the mediator.

Mediation in action continued

3 DEFINE PROBLEM
Although you will strive to remain open to new suggestions once the actual three-way meeting takes place, you should at this stage try to describe what you see as the main sticking point between the protagonists. Write it down and try and summarize it in two or three sentences. For instance,

■ X likes to be in control of a project, to be on top of each stage, and to meet deadlines even if the best quality work hasn't been delivered in the belief that timing is as important as achieving the best possible result.

■ Y, on the other hand, has a far less systematic way of working and delivers work invariably late. When he does deliver, the work is of high quality but the customer is frustrated by the lateness.

4 EXPLAIN ROLE OF MEDIATOR
Briefly explain to both protagonists that you won't offer opinions on the conflict. You will merely try to steer dialog toward agreement.

5 ESTABLISH MEETING TIME/PLACE
Finally, having accepted the mediating task, arrange a suitable time for all three of you to attend a meeting and choose a meeting place that is as neutral as possible. Don't meet in a place that is more familiar to one than the other.

Mediation in action continued

THE MEETING:

1 START TOGETHER

Much of the success of the meeting will depend on the two aggrieved parties feeling that you the mediator are being fair. You have to establish your neutrality from the start so if one of the parties arrives earlier than the other, don't start discussing the conflict before the third person arrives. If one of the protagonists is there first and tries to lure you into a debate, make it clear that you are not prepared to discuss the matter further. Stick to pleasantries or generalities.

2 INTRODUCE THE MEETING

Once the three of you are present, it is up to you to take the initiative and make a formal introduction of the meeting. Even if you have already explained the role of a mediator to them in your preliminary meetings, repeat it. Then, you can summarize why you have been asked to act as a mediator. Keep it general. For instance: "I have been asked to mediate between X and Y to try and help them reach an agreement." If you are more specific at this stage, you are in danger of formulating the problem in a way that seems to sympathize more with one party than the other. To return to the original example, this formulation, for instance, would be wrong: "We are here to discuss Y's constant lateness with his work and the way his missed deadlines are causing pressure at work." This appears to side completely with one party's perception of the problem.

Mediation in action continued

3 ESTABLISH GUIDELINES

Although the participants will be doing the work to come to an agreement, you are there to steer matters. Lay down the ground rules. To start with, say that you have all agreed that you will remain at the meeting until, hopefully, a breakthrough is achieved. This may take half an hour, although, more likely, it will take two to three hours. It may not happen at all in a first meeting. However, the protagonists should be aware of how much time, approximately, you are expecting the meeting to take. The mediator will also explain that each protagonist will speak in turn and that they are not to interrupt each other. Each person will be allotted a specific timeframe in which to outline his or her case, say, 10 to 15 minutes at the most. There will be some space for questions before further discussions can take place.

4 LET THEM TELL THEIR STORY

If both parties have requested the meeting, you may have to toss a coin to see who is first to recount his or her side of the story. If one particular member has pushed for the meeting, allow that person to begin. Do your best not to interrupt during each speech, even if you are burning to ask more questions. Be scrupulously fair in sticking to timings, even if one party wants to continue, or seems to have a longer story. In many cases, a long story is simply restating what has already been said.

Mediation in action continued

5 BE ALERT TO NEGATIVES/POSITIVES

While each person is speaking, take notes and circle any areas that you see as significantly contentious and that are likely to act as major obstacles. Similarly, circle any words or phrases that seem to reflect a more positive attitude. For instance, if one speaker is criticizing the other's behavior but makes a passing positive statement, home in on this goodwill gesture and come back to it during the discussion stage. Conciliatory gestures include:

■ Any apologies

■ Any admission of responsibility

■ Any concessions

■ Any compliments, however faint

You may be able to refer back to these later or ask them to elaborate on any of these positives. Encouraging goodwill can only help in the later stage of coming to an agreement.

6 PARAPHRASE

As well as spotting any positive signals from one or the other toward their supposed opponent, keep showing the protagonists that you are actively listening to them by restating what they have told you, in a couple of brief sentences. For instance: "What you seem to be saying is that every time Y continues to hand in work late, the client is on the phone to you, and you have to make up excuses for the delay. Is that correct?" The original accusation may have been rather long winded and told in a highly emotional state, losing its impact on the other party. By stating the complaint in such a matter-of-fact tone, you may help to communicate to the other person just how his lack of punctuality is hurting the business.

The person may never have looked at his lateness in this light. He just thought that he was being picked on unfairly. He might not have seen the consequences of his actions.

Mediation in action continued

7 IDENTIFY COMMON GOALS
Try to highlight goals that both sides have in common. To
continue the dispute on late delivery vs. high-quality work,
you can show both protagonists how they are both striving
for the same thing: "to keep clients satisfied." If one side wants
to deliver work on time and the other insists on producing
work only of the highest quality, you can explain that both
these goals are not mutually exclusive. If they are acting as a
team, they should be able to fulfill both objectives by trying
to devise a working pattern that will ensure both deliver
what they want.

8

AGREE ON COMPROMISES

By underlining common denominators and objectives, you are gradually moving toward a way that both parties can alter some part of their behavior for the greater good of the team or the project. Make sure it is specific. "We have to make sure that the customer gets the product on time and in perfect shape" is more goal-oriented than a vague "We will try to work better together." One side has to agree to put a greater emphasis on achieving a top-quality product while the other has to learn the importance of delivering work on time.

Ending the meeting

There are typically, three possible outcomes to a mediation session:

1 AGREE
The ideal scenario is for a mediation session to end with a concrete agreement or resolution:

- Clarify the wording of the agreement. For instance, assuming the agreement is about producing high quality work to schedule, describe it simply as "to deliver the best quality product on time."

- Establish markers or measurements that ensure that both parties are adhering to the agreement. For instance: "all products must be examined by quality control specialist for approval and all products must be delivered by a certain hour/day of the week in time to ensure delivery by the end of the week."

- Put agreement and markers in writing.

- Ask both parties to sign the agreement.

- Thank all parties for attending the mediation session.

2
ARRANGE FURTHER MEDIATION

You may have got close to reaching an agreement by the end of the session but are unable to overcome a couple of sticking points. However, you may sense that these obstacles may disappear after a further meeting so cut your losses at this first session and agree to meet again for a second mediation meeting. Don't put off the next meeting for too long or you will lose the momentum. If you are unable to agree on certain points, at least end the session, having agreed on a date for the next meeting.

3
ACCEPT TERMINATION

Either as a result of a disastrous first meeting or after a series of further mediation sessions, there are some occasions when a mediator has to be totally honest and admit that there is no possible way to break the deadlocks, at least in the present circumstances. You may decide to simply "terminate" the mediation process or at least, to pass on to a second mediator. Often these types of cases then move on to arbitration if they are commercial disputes. More personal conflicts may end up building up further tension or one of the parties may be forced to resign from their post.

Key questions: Making mediation work

1 WHAT IS MEDIATION?
Mediation is a form of assisted negotiation whereby the two conflicting parties willingly turn to a third-party observer to oversee the ongoing dispute.

2 WHAT ARE THE BENEFITS OF MEDIATION?
- Encourages decision-making
- Can speed up resolution
- Is cost-effective

3 WHEN IS MEDIATION SUITABLE?
- If you are ready to invest time and energy in resolving the conflict
- If you want to avoid a legal battle
- If you are flexible about the final outcome

4 WHO MEDIATES?
- Business colleagues/associates
- Managers
- Consultants
- Lawyer/accountants

5

WHAT ARE IDEAL CHARACTERISTICS OF THE MEDIATOR?
- Expert in field
- Partial observer
- Good listener
- Strategic thinker

6

WHAT ARE THE MAIN STAGES OF MEDIATION?

PREPARING THE MEDIATION. Only when both sides are convinced about the usefulness of mediation can they choose the mediator. A mediator must have some sense of the conflict and its protagonists to evaluate quickly whether he or she thinks it is worth his or her time and energy to go ahead.

THE MEETING. The mediator should make a formal introduction of the meeting and lay down ground rules. He or she should also take notes and paraphrase the positions, trying to highlight goals that both sides have in common. Finally, he or she should steer both parties towards compromise.

ENDING THE MEETING. There are three possible outcomes:
- Agree: this is the ideal scenario.
- Arrange for a further mediation session.
- Terminate the mediation process or, at least, to pass it on to a second mediator.

KEY QUESTIONS

Conclusion

As a manager, you will find conflict in the workplace unavoidable. The key is to accept this fact, and work out strategies for dealing with it. Conflict occurs for a number of reasons and in all sort of situations, between people of equal rank in an organization, and between managers and subordinates. This book is not intended to help you avoid conflict, but to help you accept that there are huge positives to conflict, when handled well, and deal with it effectively and equitably when it does occur.

Conflict is costly, in both financial and human terms. Accessing the information in Chapter 2 should leave you in no doubt over the need to minimize its impact in your organization. With these costs in mind, Chapter 3 provides an overview of ways to avoid conflict, by anticipating it in organizational and human terms and by creating an atmosphere in which a motivated team has the desire to work together.

Just as there are many ways in which a conflict can be resolved, so too are there many obstacles to conflict resolution. These are the subject of Chapter 4. If you know what you are likely to face when you as a manager do attempt to resolve conflict or want to facilitate the way for people to resolve conflict for themselves, you are more likely to succeed in your efforts when the time comes to put your skills into practice.

Chapter 5 is intended as a look-up facility for conflict resolution strategies in many different situations. While this book suggests that collaboration is usually the most effective way forward and presents a step-by-step guide to making it work, it is not the only plan, so other approaches are also considered. No two conflicting situations are ever the same, but many have common features, and the principles that have been outlined here should enable you to select the most appropriate

course of action for your current conflict situation in your workplace.

Finally, it is a fact of life that sometimes resolving a conflict "in house" is not possible, so Chapter 6 presents a guide to mediation—letting a third party help people in conflict to find a way forward for themselves.

Armed with the strategies presented in these pages, you should be in a good position to recognize, avoid, and resolve conflict in your organization, and if you cannot do so, accept that outside help may be needed, and choose and use mediators and arbitrators to good effect.

Index